P/D

D1562203

ANGELOS
SIKELIANOS
SELECTED POEMS

THE LOCKERT LIBRARY OF POETRY IN TRANSLATION
EDITORIAL ADVISER, JOHN FREDERICK NIMS
For other titles in the Lockert Library see page 151

ANGELOS SIKELIANOS
SELECTED POEMS

TRANSLATED AND INTRODUCED
BY EDMUND KEELEY AND
PHILIP SHERRARD

PRINCETON UNIVERSITY PRESS

Copyright © 1979 by Edmund Keeley and Philip Sherrard

Published by Princeton University Press, Princeton, New Jersey

All Rights Reserved

Library of Congress Cataloging in Publication Data will be
found on the last printed page of this book

The preparation of this translation was made possible, in part, by a
grant from the Program for Translations of the National Endowment
for the Humanities, an independent Federal Agency

The Greek text is based on the Savidis edition published by Ikaros,
Athens, 1966-68

The Lockert Library of Poetry in Translation is supported by
a bequest from the late Lacy Lockert, scholar and translator of
Corneille, Racine, and Dante

Clothbound editions of Princeton University Press books
are printed on acid-free paper, and binding materials are
chosen for strength and durability

Printed in the United States of America by Princeton
University Press, Princeton, New Jersey

Designed by Laury A. Egan

FOR OUR FRIEND
ZISSIMOS LORENZATOS

CONTENTS

OTHER BOOKS BY THE TRANSLATORS

EDMUND KEELEY

The Libation
Six Poets of Modern Greece (with Philip Sherrard)
The Gold-Hatted Lover
Vassilis Vassilikos: The Plant, The Well, The Angel
    (with Mary Keeley)
George Seferis: Collected Poems, 1924-1955
    (with Philip Sherrard)
The Impostor
C. P. Cavafy: Passions and Ancient Days
    (with George Savidis)
Modern Greek Writers (ed. with Peter Bien)
Voyage to a Dark Island
C. P. Cavafy: Selected Poems (with Philip Sherrard)
Odysseus Elytis: The Axion Esti (with George Savidis)
C. P. Cavafy: Collected Poems (with Philip Sherrard)
Cavafy's Alexandria: Study of a Myth in Progress
Ritsos in Parentheses

PHILIP SHERRARD

Orientation and Descent
The Marble Threshing Floor
The Greek East and the Latin West
Athos: The Mountain of Silence
Six Poets of Modern Greece (with Edmund Keeley)
Constantinople: The Iconography of a Sacred City
The Pursuit of Greece (editor)
Byzantium
George Seferis: Collected Poems, 1924-1955
    (with Edmund Keeley)
Modern Greece (with John Campbell)
C. P. Cavafy: Selected Poems (with Edmund Keeley)
Essays in Neohellenism (in Greek)
W. B. Yeats and the Search for Tradition
C. P. Cavafy: Collected Poems (with Edmund Keeley)
Christianity and Eros
Church, Papacy and Schism
The Wound of Greece

ACKNOWLEDGMENTS

We are indebted to the Columbia Translation Center for a prize in support of this translation. Edmund Keeley expresses his gratitude to the National Endowment for the Humanities and the Ingram Merrill Foundation for grants in aid of his work. We also wish to acknowledge the kindness of Anna Sikelianos in allowing us the right both to translate and to reproduce the Greek texts included in this volume. As in the past, Jerry Sherwood of Princeton University Press encouraged our enterprise from its inception, and Zissimos Lorenzatos, Robert Fagles, Liadain Sherrard, and Rachel Hadas gave us valuable suggestions during its course. Translations from this volume have appeared in *Canto, Sequoia, The Charioteer, Translation, The Ontario Review, Pequod, Footprint Magazine*, and *The Malahat Review*.

INTRODUCTION

ANGELOS SIKELIANOS (1884-1951) is a traditional poet in both the craft and thought that he gave to his art, more so perhaps than Cavafy, who was twenty years his senior, and Seferis, who was by fewer years his junior. Broadly speaking, there are two main aspects to his poetry: on the one hand, the lyrical affirmation of the natural world and of the human body as part of it, and on the other, the vision of the seer who knows that the natural world is doomed to tragic suffering and who aspires "to rise above this flesh-consuming rhythm" in order to find fulfillment in another order of reality. There is the celebration of all life's forms and sensual energies, and there is that contemplative, sometimes almost mystical intensity which transcends the merely temporal and fugitive. Both these aspects belong to the total experience of the poetry, and we have kept them in mind in making our choices for this volume, as we did for our earlier, more limited selection in *Six Poets of Modern Greece* (1960). The versions which appeared in that selection have now been completely revised.

Sikelianos's early work for the most part expresses the lyrical affirmation of the natural world and its beauty. The vision is in one sense simple, direct, unaffected, yet it is also highly metaphoric and syntactically complicated. One is reminded of some of the "nature" poetry of Dylan Thomas. In both poets there is an intimate and dynamic relationship between the poet and his "local habitation," in Sikelianos's case, the land and seas of Greece. Nature and natural forms are felt to share in the poet's own subjective experience; the force that feeds the one feeds the other:

> The sea's sound floods my veins,
> above me the sun
> grinds like a millstone,
> the wind beats its full wings,
> the world's axle throbs heavily.

xiii

I cannot hear my deepest breath,
and the sea grows calm to the sand's edge
and spreads deep inside me.

or again:

As in a glass hive my soul moved inside me,
    a joyful bee-swarm
that, secretly increasing, seeks to release into the trees
    its grapelike cluster.

And I felt the earth was crystal beneath my feet,
    the soil transparent,
for the strong and peaceful bodies of tall plane trees
    rose up around me.

Yet this world—this physical configuration of the earth, the
seas and sky of Greece—is not simply natural. It is also full
of divinities. The horse on which the poet rides at sunset to
the top of the red rock of Acrocorinth—

Was it the hour? The rich odors?
Was it the sea's deep saltiness?
The forest's breathing far away?

—is also, "had the meltemi held strong / a little longer," the
mythic Pegasus. And the he-goat that in the burning midday
heat moves away from the herd to stand on the edge of the
shore opposite Salamis, "upper lip pulled back so that his
teeth shone . . . / huge, erect, smelling the white-crested
sea / until sunset," captures in the majesty of his goatish
form the vitality of Pan.

In other words, implicit even in these early poems is what
one might call a mythological or metaphysical attitude toward
life. There is a supernatural world as well as a natural world,
there is the invisible as well as the visible. According to
Sikelianos, everything in the natural and visible world when
rightly perceived can be seen as the expression of the supernatural and the invisible. All is a manifestation of an original
divine life and is therefore holy. At the same time, when man's

vision is unpurified or "uninitiated," man usually regards everything as existing in its own right and apart from the divine, a perspective that implies disunity, a disintegration or dismemberment of the original wholeness of things. The task of the man with true knowledge and insight—the task of the prophet, the sage, or the visionary poet—is to restore this lost unity and to reconcile natural with supernatural, visible with invisible, first in his own life and then by making others aware of their divided state. As the poet phrases it in "Daedalus," for the prophet, sage, and visionary poet

> . . . the earth and the heavens are one
> and our own thought is the world's hearth and center,
> since we also say that earth may mingle with the stars
> as a field's subsoil with its topsoil, so that the heavens too
> may bring forth wheat . . .

In these symbolic terms Sikelianos expresses both the existential fact of man's living in a kind of sundered reality—time separated from eternity, flesh from spirit—and also the possibility of this dichotomy being healed through an act of creative understanding and mediation.

The source of this view of life appears to have been two-fold, or at least to have a dual character. In the first instance, Sikelianos derived it from the Greek people and their traditions, from the village pattern of life that still flourished in the poet's childhood. There he found an ancient soul and an ancient aura. And there he found a vital reality to sustain his art. How richly Sikelianos was able to draw on images and rituals enshrined in the lives of the Greek people is evident from his long poem "The Village Wedding," which is but one of his many poems that spring from the same source.

But Sikelianos did not regard the Greek people as the originators of the beliefs and practices to which they still adhered. On the contrary, he saw their traditions as the rapidly disappearing reflection of a far more universal and ancient form of wisdom, the oral library, so to speak, of Greece's most profound culture. Their beliefs were a relic of a former knowledge. Their collective memory was a repository of images and symbols whose source lay in a fully articulated metaphysical tradition. Sikelianos increasingly came to see this tradition, in its Greek form, as most adequately embodied in the pre-Socratic world. The vision of the pre-Socratics, he felt, was free from those dichotomies that to a greater or lesser extent have fragmented later systems. Then, the metaphysician did not stifle the poet or the poet the human being. Nature and the supernatural were linked together inseparably, aspects of life's organic wholeness in which such divisions were surpassed. Sikelianos regarded Orphism and the cult of Dionysus, the teachings of Pythagoras, the Mysteries of Eleusis, and the mantic center at Delphi as four of the main expressions of this tradition. In these he found a shared vision that proclaimed not only the brotherhood of all men but of all living creatures and that placed man as the channel of communication between higher and lower states of existence, between the visible and the invisible. And he believed this tradition was not incompatible with that of Christianity, the actual religion of the Greek people for most of the past two thousand years. Sikelianos saw both traditions as enshrining what is essentially the same wisdom. Two of his finest long poems, "Easter of the Greeks" and "Mother of God," move authoritatively within a completely Christian ethos, while the poem with which we conclude the present selection, "Agraphon," is based on an unrecorded episode in the life of the Christian Savior. Indeed, Sikelianos felt no embarrassment in invoking "my Christ and my Dionysus" in a single breath. Yet it is the pre-Socratic tradition that remains archetypal for him.

Of particular importance for Sikelianos was the role of poetry and of the poet in the ancient tradition that influenced him most. It was something of the same role that he himself aspired to fill in modern Greece: the poet standing at the center of his world as inspired prophet and seer, teacher and mystagogue. Sikelianos considered Pindar and Aeschylus to be the two poets of ancient Greece who best fulfilled this definition of the poet's role. And they fulfilled it through their use of myth, myth understood not as a rhetorical or metaphorical device but as a spontaneous creation of the human soul directed toward the revelation of a hidden spiritual life. In this context, Sikelianos quoted Schelling with approval: "Mythology contains within it all religious truth. Religion is not mythology, as modern scholars imagine. On the contrary, mythology is religion. All myths are true. They are not fabrications about what does not exist, but revelations of what always exists. Persephone of the Mysteries of Eleusis does not merely symbolize, but is truly, for those who can understand her, a living being. The same can be said where all the gods are concerned." The same can also be said for all those divine or semidivine figures whom Sikelianos invokes in his poetry, for his use of myth is essentially in keeping with the significance that Schelling attributes to it.

Given Sikelianos's conception of the poet as seer, as agent for bringing into close communion the mortal and the divine, it is not surprising to find that his persona—the first-person voice that is the dominant one in his poems—often seems larger than life, almost a force in nature that transcends humanity, the voice for rhetoric that is divinely inspired:

And there, from my being's depths, from the depths
where a god lay hidden in my mind's shadow,
the holy delirium was now set free,
and from the obscurity of my silences
powerful verses suddenly engulfed
my brain . . .

The persona often assumes the manner and dress of a priest, an ascetic who has been initiated into the mysteries and who can address the gods and even their grand earthly habitations directly:

O Taygetus,
bronze mountain,
at last you receive me as an ascetic!

what new impulses
nourished my untamable and silent strength,

veil of the tumult on your five peaks
where the snow was slowly thawing,

aerial cataracts
of the flowering oleander
on the escarpments,

dawning of the Doric Apollo
before my eyes,
O harsh sculptured form
on the red unsoftened bronze!

This hierophantic, rhapsodic voice is possibly the one least accessible to a contemporary Western sensibility, not only because that sensibility has been trained in our time to question rhetoric of almost any kind, but because the voice depends for credibility and vitality on the character of the language it offers, on the resonances and surprises that Sikelianos's quite magnificent use of demotic brings to the Greek reader—all of which is lost in translation. When the voice succeeds in the original (and it does not always), it is likely to fail in English to some degree.

There is evidence in Sikelianos's later poems that during the latter part of his life the poet went through a personal crisis marked by suffering and that the subsequent catharsis brought both a new humility and a renewed sense of his mission. There is also evidence that the poet's growth in the years immediately before the Second World War prepared him to understand and confront his country's cruel fate during the war years with a kind of prophetic wisdom more profound than anything in his previous poetry. At all events, during this period the rhapsodic voice surrenders to a voice in which the poet, combining the subjective and the narrative, speaks with a solemn, tragic dignity. This voice is represented in our selection by the poems "Daedalus," "The Sacred Way" and, above all perhaps, "Agraphon," the latter written during the devastating Athenian autumn of 1941 under the German occupation of Greece. In these poems the poet is no longer the hierophant transmitting a godly message through priestly rhetoric. He allows the myth at the poem's center to have its own life through narrative exposition, then brings himself into the myth by analogy, sharing its significance, joining his own experience of suffering and commitment to its revelation, but holding his focus on what the myth has already established. In this way the personal dimension does not overwhelm the metaphorical, and the subjective rhetoric in the poem becomes transformed into the universal and sublime.

Sikelianos was a prolific writer by comparison with Cavafy and Seferis. Along with the three volumes of collected poems that he published under the title *Lyrical Life*, he wrote several plays in verse and a considerable number of essays on various themes. And in contrast to both Cavafy and Seferis, a substantial number of his poems are over ten pages long ("The Village Wedding" and "Artemis Orthia" in our selection are among these). Three of the longest poems, "Mother of God," "Easter of the Greeks," and "Delphic Song," are considered to be among his major poems; but since two of them are written in decapentasyllabic couplets (the traditional meter of modern Greek folk poetry) and the third in equally formal quatrains, it proved impossible for us to offer a just representation of these in English. Sikelianos was a formal poet in the sense that he never wrote in free verse, and he often turned to the sonnet form (our selection includes six sonnets) or other strict forms of his own devising. We have not attempted to duplicate any of his forms literally, but we have tried to offer a metrical equivalent in each instance, with a loose blank verse the prevailing form in the rendering of his later poems. Our selection has been dictated more than anything else by a sense of justice both to the original and to the English language: we have not included any work that seems to us to treat the original harshly, and we have tried to limit our choice to those translations that have some life of their own in English. The selection has been severe, and for this reason it may not give the image of the poet that Sikelianos himself would have preferred: that of the sleepless artificer (his own term) with a lifelong commitment to the role of poet-prophet in the tradition of Pindar and Aeschylus or, in more recent

times, of Hölderlin, Yeats, and St. John Perse. But we hope
that what we offer here is sufficient to exemplify the sensibility, aspiration, and achievement that make Sikelianos one
of the major Greek poets of his century.

KATOUNIA, LIMNI, EVIA
SUMMER 1978

THE POEMS

ΓΥΡΙΣΜΟΣ

Ὕπνος ἱερός, λιονταρίσιος,
τοῦ γυρισμοῦ, στὴ μεγάλη
τῆς ἀμμουδιᾶς ἁπλωσιά.
Στὴν καρδιά μου
τὰ βλέφαρά μου κλεισμένα·
καὶ λάμπει, ὡσὰν ἥλιος, βαθιά μου . . .

Βοὴ τοῦ πελάου πλημμυρίζει
τὶς φλέβες μου·
ἀπάνω μου τρίζει
σὰ μυλολίθαρο ὁ ἥλιος·
γεμάτες χτυπάει τὶς φτεροῦγες ὁ ἀγέρας·
ἀγκομαχάει τὸ ἄφαντο ἀξόνι.
Δὲ μοῦ ἀκούγεται ἡ τρίσβαθη ἀνάσα.
Γαληνεύει, ὡς στὸν ἄμμο, βαθιά μου
καὶ ἁπλώνεται ἡ θάλασσα πᾶσα.

Σὲ ψηλοθόλωτο κύμα
τὴν ὑψώνει τὸ ἀπέραντο χάδι·
ποτίζουν τὰ σπλάχνα
τὰ ὁλόδροσα φύκια,

2

RETURN

Holy, lionlike sleep
of the return, on the sand's
vast spaciousness.
In my heart my eyelids closed;
and radiance, like a sun, fills me.

The sea's sound floods my veins,
above me the sun
grinds like a millstone,
the wind beats its full wings;
the world's axle throbs heavily.
I cannot hear my deepest breath,
and the sea grows calm to the sand's edge
and spreads deep inside me.

The infinite caress exalts it
into a high-domed wave;
the cool seaweed
freshens me deep down;

3

ραντίζει τα διάφωτη ἡ ἄχνα
τοῦ ἀφροῦ ποὺ ξεσπάει στὰ χαλίκια·
πέρα σβήνει τὸ σύφυλλο βούισμα
ὁποὺ ξέχειλο ἀχοῦν τὰ τζιτζίκια.

Μιά βοὴ φτάνει ἀπόμακρα·
καὶ ἄξαφνα,
σὰν πανὶ τὸ σκαρμὸ ποὺ ἔχει φύγει,
χτυπάει· εἶν' ὁ ἀγέρας ποὺ σίμωσε,
εἶν' ὁ ἥλιος ποὺ δεῖ μπρὸς στὰ μάτια μου
— καὶ ὁ ἁγνὸς ὄχι ξένα τὰ βλέφαρα
στὴν ὑπέρλευκην ὄψη του ἀνοίγει.

Πετιῶμαι ἀπάνω. Ἡ ἀλαφρότη μου
εἶναι ἴσια μὲ τὴ δύναμή μου.
Λάμπει τὸ μέτωπό μου ὁλόδροσο,
στὸ βασίλεμα σειέται ἀνοιξάτικο
βαθιὰ τὸ κορμί μου.
Βλέπω γύρα. Τὸ Ἰόνιο,
καὶ ἡ ἐλεύτερη γῆ μου!

4

the foam's lucid spindrift
breaks into spray on the pebbles;
beyond, where the cicadas stridulate,
the leaves' rustle dies away.

From far off comes a sound
that suddenly beats,
as a sail when the yardarm breaks:
it is the wind approaching,
it is the sun setting before me—
and one who is pure opens to its white presence
eyes that are kindred to it.

I leap up. My lightness
is equal to my strength.
My cool forehead glows,
in the spring sunset
my body stirs deeply.
I gaze around me: the Ionian sea,
and my delivered land!

Τ' ΑΛΟΓΑ ΤΟΥ ΑΧΙΛΛΕΑ

Ὦ ἀσφοδελώνα· δίπλα σου
δυὸ ἐχλιμιντρίσαν ἄλογα
καὶ διάβηκαν τρεχάτα . . .
Σὰν κύμα ἔλαμπ' ἡ ράχη τους·
ἀπὸ τὸ πέλαο βήκανε,
τὸν ἔρμο ἄμμο ἐσκίσανε,
μὲ ὀρτοὺς λαιμούς, τετράψηλα,
μὲ ἄσπρους ἀφρούς, βαρβάτα . . .
Στὰ μάτια τους κουφόκαιγε
μιὰν ἀστραψιά· καὶ βύθισαν
πάλι στὸ κύμα, κύματα,
ἀφρὸς στοῦ πέλαου τὸν ἀφρό,
καὶ χάθηκαν. Καὶ γνώρισα
τ' ἄτια, ποὺ τό 'να ἀνθρώπινη
φωνὴν ἐπῆρε μάντισσα.
Τὰ ἡνία ἐκράτει ὁ ἥρωας·
χτύπησε, ἐτράβηξε μπροστὰ
τὰ θεοτικά του νιάτα . . .

Ἄτια ἱερά, ἀκατάλυτα
σᾶς κράτησεν ἡ μοίρα,
στὰ μέτωπα τὰ ὁλόμαυρα
δένοντας, γιὰ τὰ βέβηλα
τὰ μάτια, μιὰν ὁλόλευκη
μεγάλη ἀβασκαντήρα!

6

THE HORSES OF ACHILLES *

Field of asphodels, beside you
two horses neighed
as they went by at a gallop.
Their backs gleamed like a wave;
they came up out of the sea,
tore over the deserted sand,
necks straining high, towering,
white foam at the mouth, stallion-strong.
In their eyes
lightning smoldered;
and, waves themselves, they plunged again
into the waves,
foam into the sea's foam,
and vanished. I recognized
those stallions: one of them
took on a human voice to prophesy.
The hero held the reins;
he spurred, hurling
his godlike youth forward. . .

Sacred stallions, fate
has kept you indestructible,
fixing on your pure black foreheads,
charm against the profane eye,
a large and pure white talisman.

ΣΠΑΡΤΗ

« Ἔχω καιρὸ ποὺ σοῦ φυλάω καρτέρι·
ἀνάμεσ᾽ ἀπ᾽ τοὺς ἄλλους, μὲ τὸ μάτι
σ᾽ ἐδιάλεξα, σὰ νά 'σουνα τὸ ἀστέρι·
μὄχει ἡ θωριά σου τὴν καρδιὰ χορτάτη.

» Ἄκου . . . Ἄς σοῦ σφίγγω δυνατὰ τὸ χέρι·
τὰ νιάτα ἔτσι δαμάζονται, σὰν ἄτι . . .
Γιὰ μιὰ νυχτιά, τῆς γυναικός μου ἀιταίρι
θὰ γείρεις, στὸ δικό μου τὸ κρεβάτι!

» Τράβα . . . Βαθύζωνη εἶναι καὶ δεμένη
στὴν ὀμορφιὰ σὰν τὴν ψηλὴν Ἑλένη . . .
Γιόμοσ᾽ τη ἐσὺ μὲ τὸ γενναῖο σου σπέρμα . . .

» Στὸ δυνατὸν ἀγκάλιασμά σου πάρ᾽ τη,
γιὰ μιὰ νυχτιά, καὶ σκῶσε ὀμπρὸς στὴ Σπάρτη,
μ᾽ ἄξιον ὑγιό, τὰ γερατειά μου τὰ ἔρμα!»

8

SPARTA*

"A long time now I've lain in wait for you;
my eye singled you out from all the others
as though you lived among them like a star;
your grace and beauty gratify my heart.

Listen—let me grip your hand firmly:
youth is tamed that way, like a stallion—
for a single night, in my own bed,
you will be partner to my wife!

Go. She is slim-waisted, a woman
pledged to beauty as tall Helen was.
Go, fill her with your generous seed.

Take her in your powerful embrace
for one night only, and in Sparta's eyes,
through a worthy son, exalt my dry old age."

ΔΩΡΙΚΟ

Μὲ κόμη θερισμένη ὡς τὸν αὐχένα,
σὰν τοῦ Δωριέα ᾿Απόλλωνα, τὰ μέλη
στὴ στενὴ κλίνη ἐκράτει παγωμένα
μὲς σὲ βαριὰ ἀξεδιάλυτη νεφέλη . . .

῎Αδειασ᾿ ἡ ᾿Αρτέμιδα ὅλα της τὰ βέλη.
Καὶ λίγο ἀκόμα ἂν ἤτανε παρθένα,
τὴν ἡδονὴ κλειδώνανε, σφιγμένα,
σὰν κρύα κερήθρα, τὰ παρθένα σκέλη . . .

Καθὼς στοῦ στίβου μέσα τὸν ἀγώνα,
᾿πίθων᾿ ὁ νιὸς ἀπάνω της τὸ γόνα
μύρα ἀλειμμένος, ὅπως γιὰ τὴν πάλη . . .

Κι ἂν ἔσπαε τῶν χεριῶν της τ᾿ ἀντιστύλια,
μά ᾿ργειαν πολὺ μ᾿ ὅμοια κραυγὴ τὰ χείλια
νὰ σμίξουν, κι ἀπ᾿ τοὺς ἴδρωτες ἡ ἀγκάλη! . . .

10

DORIC

Her hair curled in at the nape of her neck
like the Doric Apollo's hair, she kept*
her limbs frozen on the narrow bed
in a heavy, indissoluble cloud.

Artemis fired all her arrows at her.
And though she soon would cease to be a virgin,
still her virgin legs, like a cold honeycomb,
sealed in her sensual joy.

As if in combat in the ring,
he knelt, his body oiled with myrrh,
to press her as a wrestler might.

And though he breached her outthrust arms
it was some time before they locked their lips,
cried out as one, and in their sweat embraced . . .

11

Η ΠΑΝΑΓΙΑ ΤΗΣ ΣΠΑΡΤΗΣ

Ἀπὸ χαλκὸν ἢ βράχο Πεντελίσιο
τὸ ἀθάνατο εἴδωλό Σου δὲ θὰ στήσω·
μ' ἀπὸ κυπαρισσόξυλο κολόνα,
γιὰ νὰ εὐωδάει τὸ ἔργο μου στὸν αἰώνα!...

Καὶ στὸ λόφον, ὁπόχει ὅμοια κορόνα
τὸ κάστρο τὸ Βενέτικο, θὰ χτίσω
βαριὰ ἐκκλησιά, καὶ μέσα θὰ Σὲ κλείσω
μ' ἀτάραγο, ἀπὸ σίδερο, πυλώνα!

Καμπάνες, ποὺ νὰ βόγκουνε ὡς ἀσπίδα
πὄβρει σὲ σπάθα ἢ κονταριοῦ κοπίδα,
θὰ βάλω, κι ἄλλες πιὸ ψηλά, σὰ σεῖστρα!

Κι ἀπ' τὰ παράθυρά της νὰ Σὲ ἰσκιάσω,
βαθύχρωμα κρουστάλλια θὰ ταιριάσω
— καὶ τὸ καθένα νά 'ναι πολεμίστρα!

THE HOLY VIRGIN OF SPARTA

Neither in bronze nor in Pendelic rock
will I shape Your undying image
but from a column of cypress wood
so that my work will give its scent forever.

And on the hill where a Venetian castle*
sits like a crown, I will build you a church—
heavy, solid—and close you inside it,
the gates impenetrable, made of iron.

There will be bells to echo like a shield
struck by a saber or lance's point,
and higher up, bells like sistra.

And in the windows, to bring You shade,
I will fashion glass of the deepest colors
—and may each serve for an embrasure.

ΣΤΟΝ ΑΚΡΟΚΟΡΙΝΘΟ

Στὸν Ἀκροκόρινθο ἔπεφτεν ἡ δύση
πυρώνοντας τὸ βράχο. Κ' εὐωδάτη
φυκιοῦ πνοή, ἀπ' τὸ πέλαο, εἶχε ἀρχίσει
νὰ μεθᾷ τὸ λιγνὸ βαρβάτο μου ἄτι . . .

Ἀφροὶ στὸ χαλινάρι· κι ἀπ' τὸ μάτι
τ' ἀσπράδι ὅλο φαινόταν· καὶ νὰ λύσει
τὴ φούχτα μου, ἀπ' τὰ γκέμια του γεμάτη,
πάλευε πρὸς τὰ πλάτη νὰ χιμήσει . . .

Ἥτανε ἡ ὥρα; Ἦταν τὰ πλήθια μύρα;
Ἦταν βαθιὰ τοῦ πέλαγου ἡ ἁρμύρα;
ἡ ἀναπνοὴ ἡ ἀπόμακρη τοῦ δάσου;

Ἄ! λίγο ἀκόμα ἂν κράταε τὸ μελτέμι,
ἤξερα ἐγὼ πῶς σφίγγεται τὸ γκέμι
καὶ τὰ πλευρὰ τοῦ μυθικοῦ Πηγάσου!

14

ON ACROCORINTH

The sun set over Acrocorinth*
burning the rock red. From the sea
a fragrant smell of seaweed now began
to intoxicate my slender stallion.

Foam on the bit, the white of his eye
bared fully, he struggled to break
my grip, tight on his reins,
to leap free into open space.

Was it the hour? The rich odors?
Was it the sea's deep saltiness?
The forest's breathing far away?

O had the meltemi held strong*
a little longer, I would have gripped
the reins and flanks of mythic Pegasus!*

ΤΡΕΧΑΝΤΗΡΑ

Καταμεσῆς ἀνέμου ἡ τρεχαντήρα,
μὲ τὰ πανιά της τόξα τεντωμένα,
τοῦ δοιακιοῦ τὴ στερνὴν ἐπῆρε γύρα
στὰ γαλανὰ βουνὰ τὰ γυμνωμένα . . .

Κι ὁ αἰθεροδρόμος βόγκος ποὺ ἐπλημμύρα
στὰ ξάρτια, στὰ πρυμνήσια, στὴν ἀντένα
— δελφίνια παρατρέχανε ὁλοένα —
τὴν ἔκρουε μὲς στὸ κύμα, ὁλόρτη λύρα!

Δίκοπη σπάθα, ἐξέσκιζε ἡ καρίνα . . .
Κι ὁ ἀφρὸς στὴν πρύμνα, χώριος σὲ δυὸ κρίνα,
τῶν σταλιῶν ἀνατίναζε τὸ σεῖστρο . . .

Σάν, μ' ἔνα «λάσκα!» — ὁ ἥλιος μεσουράνει —
στῶν Σαλώνων ἐμπῆκε τὸ λιμάνι
μὲ τὸν καταμεσήμερο μαΐστρο!

16

CAIQUE

Caique in the wind's center,
sails hauled in bow-taut,
tiller swinging into the final tack
against the bare blue mountains.

And the heaven-coursing howl that swamped
rigging, moorings in the stern, the yard
—dolphins in pursuit all the way—
strummed her over the waves: an upright lyre.

Double-headed axe, the keel carved.
And the wake's foam, twinned as lilies,
rattled the sistrum of the wind's falling.

Then with a sudden "bear off"
—sun at its zenith—the caique found
Salona harbor in the noon's nor'wester.*

17

ΖΩΦΟΡΟΣ

Μὲ φτέρνα ὡς μῆλο κόκκινο χτυπώντας
τὰ πλευρὰ τῶν ἀλόγων, φουντωμένη
'ποὺ φλέβα κλαδωτὴ κι ὁ ἱδρὸς κολλώντας
στὴν κοιλιὰ καὶ στὰ νύχια κατεβαίνει·

καὶ μὲ τὴν ἁπαλάμη σαλαγώντας
στὸ λαιμό, 'πού 'ν' ἡ τρίχα χωρισμένη
σὰν τὸ φτερὸ τοῦ κύκνου, ἀναδεμένοι
μὲ σκιάδι ἢ μὲ στεφάνι, πᾶν' ὁρμώντας...

Ἡ γῆ στὸ κάμα ἀνοίγει... Τὸ τζιτζίκι
στὶς ἐλιὲς διαλαλεῖ μιὰ ἀνάερη νίκη...
— ἡ λιτανεία τὸν πέπλο τώρα βγάνει·

καὶ μὲ τὸ λίγο ἀγέρι φεύγει πρίμα
χορευτὸ τῶν ἀτιῶν τὸ πλούσιο κύμα,
κάλπασμα, τετραπόδισμα, ἢ ραβάνι...

18

FRIEZE*

With heels apple-red beating
the horses' flanks where veins swollen
and forked ripple, and sweat on the belly
trickles down to the hooves;

with flat palm guiding the nape
where the mane is parted in two
like a swan's wing, heads
shaded or crowned, they rush past.

Earth at red heat opens. Cicadas
in the olive trees announce an ethereal victory.
The procession now brings on the robe;

and with the light breeze astern
the great wave of horses dances forward
at a trot, canter, or gallop.

19

ΑΝΑΔΥΟΜΕΝΗ

Στὸ ρόδινο μακάριο φῶς, νά με, ἀνεβαίνω τῆς αὐγῆς,
μὲ σηκωμένα χέρια.
Ἡ θεία γαλήνη μὲ καλεῖ τοῦ πέλαου, ἔτσι γιὰ νὰ βγῶ
πρὸς τὰ γαλάζια αἰθέρια . . .

Μὰ ὦ οἱ ἄξαφνες πνοὲς τῆς γῆς, ποὺ μὲς στὰ στήθια μου χιμᾶν
κι ἀκέρια μὲ κλονίζουν!
᾿Ω Δία, τὸ πέλαγο εἶν᾿ βαρύ, καὶ τὰ λυτά μου τὰ μαλλιὰ
σὰν πέτρες μὲ βυθίζουν!

Αὖρες, τρεχᾶτε· ὦ Κυμοθόη, ὦ Γλαύκη· ἐλᾶτε, πιᾶστε μου
τὰ χέρια ἀπ᾿ τὴ μασκάλη.
Δὲν πρόσμενα, ἔτσι μονομιᾶς, παραδομένη νὰ βρεθῶ
μὲς στοῦ Ἥλιου τὴν ἀγκάλη . . .

20

APHRODITE RISING

In the blessed rose light of dawn, look how I rise,
      my arms held high.
The sea's godlike calm bids me to ascend
      into the blue air.

O but the sudden breaths of earth, filling my breasts, rousing me
      from head to foot.
O Zeus, the sea is heavy, and my loosened hair drags me
      down like a stone.

Nymphs of the breeze, hurry; Cymothoe, Glauce, come grip me
      under my arms.*
I did not think I'd find myself so suddenly caught up
      in the sun's embrace.

21

ΤΟ ΠΡΩΤΟΒΡΟΧΙ

Σκυμμένοι ἀπὸ τὸ παραθύρι...
Καὶ τοῦ προσώπου μας οἱ γύροι
ἡ ἴδια μας ἤτανε ψυχή.
Ἡ συννεφιά, χλωμὴ σὰ θειάφι,
θάμπωνε ἀμπέλι καὶ χωράφι·
ὁ ἀγέρας μέσ' ἀπὸ τὰ δέντρα
μὲ κρύφια βούιζε ταραχή·
ἡ χελιδόνα, μὲ τὰ στήθη,
γοργή, στὴ χλόη μπρὸς - πίσω ἐχύθη·
κι ἄξαφνα βρόντησε, καὶ λύθη
κρουνός, χορεύοντα ἡ βροχή!
Ἡ σκόνη πῆρ' ἀνάερο δρόμο...
Κ' ἐμεῖς, στῶν ρουθουνιῶν τὸν τρόμο,
στὴ χωματίλα τὴ βαριὰ
τὰ χείλα ἀνοίξαμε, σὰ βρύση
τὰ σπλάχνα νά μπει νὰ ποτίσει
(ὅλη εἶχεν ἡ βροχὴ ραντίσει
τὴ διψασμένη μας θωριά,
σὰν τὴν ἐλιὰ καὶ σὰν τὸ φλόμο).
κι ὁ ἕνας στ' ἀλλουνοῦ τὸν ὦμο
ρωτάαμε: «Τ' εἶναι πόχει σκίσει
τὸν ἀέρα μύρο, ὅμοιο μελίσσι;
Ἀπ' τὸν πευκιὰ τὸ κουκουνάρι,
ὁ βάρσαμος ἢ τὸ θυμάρι,
ἡ ἀφάνα ἢ ἡ ἀλυγαριά;»
Κι ἄχνισα — τόσα ἦταν τὰ μύρα —
ἄχνισα κ' ἔγινα ὅμοια λύρα,
ποὺ χάιδευ' ἡ ἄσωτη πνοή...
Μοῦ γιόμισ' ὁ οὐρανίσκος γλύκα·
κι ὡς τὴ ματιά σου ξαναβρῆκα,
ὅλο μου τὸ αἷμα ἦταν βοή!...

22

THE FIRST RAIN

We leaned out of the window.
Everything around us
was one with our soul.
Sulphur-pale, the clouds
darkened the fields, the vines;
wind moaned in the trees
with a secret turbulence,
and the quick swallow went
breasting across the grass.
Suddenly the thunder broke,
the wellhead broke,
and dancing came the rain.
Dust leaped into the air.
We, our nostrils quivering,
opened our lips to drink
the earth's heavy smell,
to let it like a spring
water us deep inside
(the rain had already wet
our thirsting faces,
like the olive and the mullen).
And shoulder touching shoulder,
we asked: "What smell is this
that cuts the air like a bee?
From balsam, pine, acanthus,
from osier or thyme?"
So many the scents that, breathing out,
I became a lyre caressed
by the breath's profusion.
Sweetness filled my palate;
and as our eyes met again
all my blood sang out.

Κ' ἔσκυψ' ἀπάνω ἀπὸ τ' ἀμπέλι
ποὺ ἐσειόνταν σύφυλλο, τὸ μέλι
καὶ τ' ἄνθι ἀκέριο νὰ τοῦ πιῶ·
— βαριὰ τσαμπιὰ καὶ οἱ λογισμοί μου.
βάτοι βαθιοὶ οἱ ἀνασασμοί μου —
κι ὅπως ἀνάσαινα, ἀπ' τὰ μύρα
δὲ μπόρεια νὰ διαλέξω ποιό!
Μὰ ὅλα τὰ μάζεψα, τὰ πῆρα,
καὶ τὰ 'πια, ὡσὰν ἀπὸ τὴ μοίρα
λύπη ἀπροσδόκητη ἢ χαρά.
Τά 'πια· κι ὡς σ' ἄγγιξα τὴ ζώνη,
τὸ αἷμα μου γίνηκεν ἀηδόνι,
κι ὡς τὰ πολύτρεχα νερά!...

24

I bent down to the vine,
its leaves shaking, to drink
its honey and its flower;
and—my thoughts like heavy grapes,
bramble-thick my breath—
I could not, as I breathed,
choose among the scents,
but culled them all, and drank them
as one drinks joy or sorrow
suddenly sent by fate;
I drank them all,
and when I touched your waist,
my blood became a nightingale,
became like the running waters.

ΠΑΝ

Στὰ βράχια τοῦ ἔρμου ἀκρογιαλιοῦ καὶ στῆς τραχιᾶς χαλικωσιᾶς
    τὴ λαύρα,
τὸ μεσημέρι, ὅμοιο πηγή, δίπλα ἀπὸ κύμα σμάραγδο,
    τρέμοντας ὅλο, ἀνάβρα' ...

Γαλάζια τριήρη στὸ βυθόν, ἀνάμεσα σ' ἐαρινοὺς ἀφρούς,
    ἡ Σαλαμίνα,
καὶ τῆς Κινέτας, μέσα μου κατάβαθος ἀνασασμός,
    πεῦκα καὶ σκίνα.

Τὸ πέλαγο ἔσκαγ' ὅλο ἀφροὺς καί, τιναχτὸ στὸν ἄνεμο,
    ἀσπροβόλα'
τὴν ὥρα ποὺ τ' ἀρίφνητο κοπάδι τῶν σιδέρικων
    γιδιῶν ροβόλα' ...

Μὲ δυὸ σουρίγματα τραχιὰ ποὺ—κάτουθε τὸ δάχτυλο
    ἀπ' τὴ γλώσσα
βάνοντας—βούιξ' ὁ μπιστικός, τὰ μάζωξ' ὅλα στὸ γιαλό,
    κι ἂς ἦταν πεντακόσα!

Κι ὅλα σταλιάσανε σφιχτὰ τριγύρ' ἀπ' τὰ κοντόθαμνα
    κι ἀπ' τὸ θυμάρι,
κι ὡς ἐσταλιάσανε, γοργά, τὰ γίδια καὶ τὸν ἄνθρωπο
    τὸ κάρωμα εἶχε πάρει.

Καὶ πιά, στὶς πέτρες τοῦ γιαλοῦ κι ἀπάνου ἀπ' τῶν σιδέρικων
    γιδιῶν τὴ λαύρα,
σιγή· κι ὡς ἀπὸ στρίποδα, μέσ' ἀπ' τὰ κέρατα, γοργὸς
    ὁ ἥλιος καπνὸς ἀνάβρα' ...

26

PAN

Over rocks on the deserted shore, over the burning heat
      of harsh pebbles,
beside the emerald waves, noon, like a fountain,
      rose shimmering.

Salamis a blue trireme deep in the sea,*
      in spring's spindrift;
the pines and mastic trees of Kineta a deep breath*
      I drew inside me.

The sea burst into foam and, beaten by the wind,
      shattered white,
and a flock of goats, countless, iron-gray, plummeted headlong
      down the hill.

With two harsh whistles, fingers pressing
      his curled tongue,
the goatherd huddled them on the shore,
      the whole five hundred.

They gathered in close, crowding the brush
      and wild thyme,
and as they gathered, a drowsiness seized
      both goats and man.

And then, over the shore's stones and the goats' swelter,
      dead silence;
and between their horns, as from a tripod, the sun's quick heat
      shimmered upward.

27

Τότε εἴδαμε—ἄρχος καὶ ταγὸς—ὁ τράγος νὰ σηκώνεται
μονάχος,
βαρὺς στὸ πάτημα κι ἀργός, νὰ ξεχωρίσει κόβοντας, κ' ἐκεῖ
ὅπου βράχος,
σφήνα στὸ κύμα μπαίνοντας, στέκει λαμπρὸ γιὰ ξάγναντο
ἀκρωτήρι,
στὴν ἄκρη ἀπάνου νὰ σταθεῖ, ποὺ ἡ ἄχνη διασκορπᾶ τ' ἀφροῦ,
κι ἀσάλευτος νὰ γείρει;

μ' ἀνασκωμένο, ἀφήνοντας νὰ λάμπουνε τὰ δόντια του,
τ' ἀπάνω χείλι,
μέγας καὶ ὀρτός, μυρίζοντας τὸ πέλαγο τὸ ἀφρόκοπο,
ὣς τὸ δείλι!

28

Then we saw the herd's lord and master, the he-goat,*
        rise alone
and move off, his tread slow and heavy,
        toward a rock

wedged into the sea to shape a perfect lookout point;
        there he stopped,
on the very edge where spray dissolves,
        and leaning motionless,

upper lip pulled back so that his teeth shone,
        he stood
huge, erect, smelling the white-crested sea
        until sunset.

29

ΘΑΛΕΡΟ

Φλογάτη, γελαστή, ζεστή, ἀπὸ τ᾽ ἀμπέλια ἀπάνωθεν
  ἐκοίταγε ἡ σελήνη·
κι ἀκόμα ὁ ἥλιος πύρωνε τὰ θάμνα, βασιλεύοντας
  μὲς σὲ διπλὴ γαλήνη.

Βαριὰ τὰ χόρτα, ἱδρώνανε στὴν ἀψηλὴν ἀπανεμιὰ
  τὸ θυμωμένο γάλα,
κι ἀπὸ τὰ κλήματα τὰ νιά, ποὺ τῆς πλαγιᾶς ἀνέβαιναν
  μακριὰ - πλατιὰ τὴ σκάλα,

σουρίζανε οἱ ἀμπελουργοὶ φτερίζοντας, ἐσειόντανε
  στὸν ὄχτο οἱ καλογιάννοι,
κι ἄπλων᾽ ἀπάνω στὸ φεγγάρι ἡ ζέστα ἀραχνοΰφαντο
  κεφαλοπάνι...

Στὸ σύρμα, μὲς στὸ γέννημα, μονάχα τρία καματερά,
  τό ᾽να ἀπὸ τ᾽ ἄλλο πίσω,
τὴν κρεμαστή τους τραχηλιὰ κουνώντας, τὸν ἀνήφορο
  ξεκόβαν τὸ βουνίσο.

Σκυφτό, τὴ γῆς μυρίζοντας, καὶ τὸ λιγνὸ λαγωνικό,
  μὲ γρήγορα ποδάρια,
στοῦ δειλινοῦ τὴ σιγαλιὰ βράχο τὸ βράχο ἐπήδαγε
  ζητώντας μου τὰ χνάρια.

Καὶ κάτου ἀπ᾽ τὴν κληματαριὰ τὴν ἄγουρη μ᾽ ἐπρόσμενε,
  στὸ ξάγναντο τὸ σπίτι,
στρωτὸ τραπέζι πὄφεγγε, λυχνάρι ὀμπρός του κρεμαστό,
  τὸ φῶς τοῦ Ἀποσπερίτη...

30

THALERO*

Glowing, festive, warm, the moon looked down
        over the vineyards
while the sun still scorched the bushes, setting
        in total stillness.

The heavy grass up on the windless height sweated
        its pungent sap
and among the new-leaved vines that climbed
        the terraced slope

the buntings fluttered and called, the robins
        hovered on the banks.
and the heat spread a fine filmy veil across
        the moon's face.

On the path between the wheat fields three oxen,
        one behind the other,
ascended the mountain slope, their pendant
        dewlaps swaying.

The slender hound, his muzzle to the earth
        in the quiet evening,
leaped from rock to rock, searching
        for my tracks.

And at the house ahead, beneath the unripe vine,
        a ready table
waited for me, a lamp hung out in front of it—
        the evening star.

Ἐκεῖ κερήθρα μόφερε, ψωμὶ σταρένιο, κρύο νερὸ
ἡ ἀρχοντοθυγατέρα,
ὁπού ’χε ἀπὸ τὴ δύναμη στὸν πετρωτό της τὸ λαιμὸ
χαράκι ὡς περιστέρα·

πού ἡ ὄψη της, σὰν τῆς βραδιᾶς τὸ λάμπο, ἔδειχνε διάφωτη
τῆς παρθενιᾶς τὴ φλόγα,
κι ἀπ’ τὴ σφιχτή της ντυμασιά, στὰ στήθια της τ’ ἀμάλαγα,
χώριζ’ ὁλόρτη ἡ ρώγα·

πού ὀμπρὸς ἀπὸ τὸ μέτωπο σὲ δυὸ πλεξοῦδες τὰ μαλλιὰ
πλεμένα εἶχε σηκώσει,
σὰν τὰ σκοινιὰ τοῦ καραβιοῦ, πού δὲ θὰ μπόρει’ ἡ φούχτα μου
νὰν τῆς τὰ χερακώσει.

Λαχανιασμένος στάθη ἐκεῖ κι ὁ σκύλος π’ ἀγανάχτησε
στὰ ὀρτὰ τὰ μονοπάτια,
κι ἀσάλευτος στὰ μπροστινά, μὲ κοίταγε, προσμένοντας
μιὰ σφήνα, μὲς στὰ μάτια.

Ἐκεῖ τ’ ἀηδόνια ὡς ἄκουγα, τριγύρα μου, καὶ τοὺς καρποὺς
γενόμουν ἀπ’ τὸ δίσκο,
εἶχα τὴ γέψη τοῦ σταριοῦ, τοῦ τραγουδιοῦ καὶ τοῦ μελιοῦ
βαθιὰ στὸν οὐρανίσκο . . .

Σὰ σὲ κυβέρτι γυάλινο μέσα μου σάλευε ἡ ψυχή,
πασίχαρο μελίσσι,
πού ὅλο κρυφὰ πληθαίνοντας γυρεύει σμάρια ὡσὰν τσαμπιὰ
στὰ δέντρα ν’ ἀμολήσει.

32

There the master's daughter brought me honeycomb, cold water,
        country bread;
her strength had engraved around her rocklike throat a circle
        like a dove's ring;

and her look, like the evening light, disclosed virginity's
        lucid flame,
and through the tight dress that covered her firm breasts the
    nipples
            stood out boldly.

Her hair was plaited in two braids
        above her forehead—
braids like the cables of a ship, too thick
        for my hand's grip.

The dog, exhausted now from the steep footpaths,
        stood there panting,
and, motionless, stared into my eyes,
        waiting for a crust.

There, as I heard the nightingale and ate fruit from the dish
        in front of me,
I had the taste of wheat, of song and honey
        deep on the palate.

As in a glass hive my soul moved inside me,
        a joyful bee-swarm
that, secretly increasing, seeks to release into the trees
        its grapelike cluster.

Κ' ἔνιωθα κρούσταλλο τὴ γῆ στὰ πόδια μου ἀποκάτωθε
καὶ διάφανο τὸ χῶμα,
γιατὶ πλατάνια τριέτικα τριγύρα μου ὑψωνόντανε
μ' ἁδρό, γαλήνιο σῶμα.

Ἐκεῖ μ' ἀνοῖξαν τὸ παλιὸ κρασί, ποὺ πλέριο εὐώδισε
μὲς στὴν ἱδρένια στάμνα,
σὰν τὴ βουνίσια μυρουδιά, σύντας βαρεῖ κατάψυχρη
νύχτια δροσιὰ τὰ θάμνα...

Φλογάτη, γελαστή, ζεστή, ἐκεῖ ἡ καρδιά μου δέχτηκε
ν' ἀναπαυτεῖ λιγάκι
πὰ σὲ σεντόνια εὐωδερὰ ἀπὸ βότανα, καὶ γαλανὰ
στὴ βάψη ἀπὸ λουλάκι...

And I felt the earth was crystal beneath my feet,
        the soil transparent,
for the strong and peaceful bodies of tall plane trees
        rose up around me.

There the old wine was opened for me, smelling rich
        in the porous jar,
as mountain scents when the cool night dew
        falls on the bushes.

Glowing, festive, warm, there my heart consented
        to repose for a while
in sheets made fragrant by herbs, azure
        by washing blue.

Η ΜΑΝΑ ΤΟΥ ΝΤΑΝΤΕ

Ἡ Φλωρεντία σὰ ν' ἄδειασε τῆς φάνη μὲς στὸν ὕπνο της,
τὸ χάραμα ὡς ἀρχίζει,
κι ἀπὸ τὶς φιλενάδες της μακριὰ τοὺς δρόμους μοναχή
νὰ σιγοσεργιανίζει . . .

Τὸ νυφικό της φόρεμα φορώντας τὸ μεταξωτό,
τὰ πέπλα τὰ κρινάτα,
τὰ σταυροδρόμια γύριζε, καὶ στ' ὄνειρο τῆς φάνταζε
καινούρια ἡ κάθε στράτα . . .

Κι ἀπὸ τοὺς λόφους πὄλουζεν ἀχνὸ ἀνοιξιάτικο αὐγινό,
σὰ μακρινὰ μελίσσια
ἀργόηχα τὰ καμπαναριὰ ξεψυχισμένα ἀχούσανε
βαθιὰ στὰ ἐρημοκλήσια . . .

Καὶ ξάφνου, σὰ νὰ βρέθηκε σὲ περιβόλι ἀνάμεσα,
μέσα στὸν ἄσπρο ἀέρα,
ντυμένο στὰ νυφιάτικα, μὲ νεραντζιὲς καὶ μὲ μηλιὲς
γεμάτο πέρα ὣς πέρα . . .

Κι ὅπως τὴ σέρναν οἱ εὐωδιές, ἕνα ψηλὸ δαφνόδεντρο
τῆς φάνη νὰ ζυγώνει,
ποὺ στὴν κορφή του ἀνέβαινε, σκαλὶ πηδώντας τὸ σκαλὶ
ἀπάνου, ἕνα παγόνι·

κ' ἐκεῖνο λύγαε τὸ λαιμὸ στό 'να καὶ στ' ἄλλο τὸ κλαδὶ
δαφνόκουκα γεμάτο,
κ' ἕνα ἔτρωγε, ἕνα τό 'παιρνε κι ἀπὸ τὸν κλῶνο τό 'ριχνε
γοργὸ στὸ χῶμα κάτω . . .

THE MOTHER OF DANTE *

In her sleep, as dawn began to break,
        it seemed that Florence had emptied
and that she was alone, far from friends,
        slowly wandering the streets.

Wearing her silk bridal gown
        and her lily-white veils
she roamed through known crossroads, and in her dream
        she imagined the roads new.

And in the hills washed by spring's dawn mist,
        like the distant sound of bees,
the belfries tolled their slow dead ring
        at secluded country chapels.

Suddenly she found herself inside a garden,
        in the white air, a garden
wearing bridal dress, with bitter-orange and apple trees
        stretching into the distance.

And as the fragrance drew her on it seemed
        a laurel tree approached,
and in it, rising step by step,
        a peacock climbed.

The peacock bent its neck from branch to branch,
        the branches rich with berries,
and sometimes ate and sometimes plucked the fruit
        to throw it to the ground.

Τὴν κεντημένη της ποδιὰν ἐσήκωσεν ἀθέλητα
στὸν ἴσκιο, μαγεμένη,
καὶ νὰ · σὲ λίγο ἐβάραινεν ἀπ᾽ τὰ σγουρὰ δαφνόκουκα
μπροστά της φορτωμένη.

Ἀπ᾽ τῆς αὐγῆς τὸν κάματο ἔτσι ἀναπαύτη μιὰ στιγμὴ
μὲς σὲ δροσάτο νέφος·
καὶ γύρα οἱ φιλενάδες της ἀπ᾽ τὸ κρεβάτι, ἐπρόσμεναν
γιὰ νὰ δεχτοῦν τὸ βρέφος!...

38

And she, against her will, held out her knitted apron
    to the shade, enraptured,
and soon she felt the weight of it in front,
    heavy with laurel berries.

She rested this way a moment from her dawn's labor
    in the coolness of a cloud;
and round the bed her women friends waited
    to receive the coming child . . .

ΠΡΟΣΕΥΧΗ

Γυμνὴ Σοῦ δέεται ἡ ψυχή. 'Απὸ χαρά, ἀπὸ πόνο
    γυμνή· ἀπὸ ἡδονὴ
γυμνὴ Σοῦ δέεται ἡ ψυχή, Δημιουργέ, μὲ μόνο
    τὴν ἄπλαστη φωνή,

πού, πρὶν στὴ σάρκα μου νὰ μπεῖ, στὸν κόρφο Σου—ὡς τζιτζίκι
    κρυμμένο στὴν ἐλιὰ—
βουλὴ δικὴ Σου χτύπαε στὴν καρδιά μου, κ' ἔλεε : «νίκη,
    νίκη στὰ πάντα!», καὶ δὲν ἤτανε μιλιὰ

δική μου, ἦταν ἡ δική Σου, Θεέ. Μ' ἐκείνη μόνο
    Σοῦ δέομαι· λύτρωσέ μου τὸ σκοπὸ
τὸ μυστικὸ ποὺ γεύτηκα βαθιὰ κ' ἔξω ἀπ' τὸ χρόνο.
    γιὰ ν' ἀγαπῶ, γιὰ ν' ἀγαπῶ

πάνω ἀπὸ πρόσωπα καὶ πλάσματα, ἀπ' τὸν ἕνα
    ποὺ κλείνω μέσα μου παλμό,
ποὺ εἶν' ἕνας πιὰ γιὰ ζωντανὰ καὶ πεθαμένα·
    δῶσε μου, ναί, τὸ λυτρωμό,

τὸν ἄναρχο Ἔρωτα νὰ νιώσω ἀκέριο, Θέ μου,
    μέσα στὰ στήθια μου ξανά·
καὶ νά 'μαι σ' ὅλα σὰν ἡ πνοὴ καὶ σὰν ἡ βοὴ τ' ἀνέμου,
    στὰ κοντινά, στὰ μακρινά...

PRAYER

Naked the soul prays to You. Stripped of joy,
        of suffering and pleasure,
naked the soul prays to You, Creator, with its
        uncreated voice alone,

that voice which, before entering my flesh, in Your breast—
        as a cicada hidden in the olive tree—
beat in my heart as Your will, crying "Victory,
        victory in all things,"

and it was not my voice, it was Yours, Lord; with that
        alone I pray to You: release in me
the secret purpose I tasted deeply outside time,
        so that I may love, may love

beyond human images and all created things, beyond the single
        pulse that throbs inside me,
one now for the living and the dead: grant me,
        grant me deliverance,

to feel again the uncreated Eros
        filling my breast,
and to be to all, to things near and far away,
        as the wind's sound and breath.

ΓΙΑΤΙ ΒΑΘΙΑ ΜΟΥ ΔΟΞΑΣΑ

Γιατὶ βαθιά μου δόξασα καὶ πίστεψα τὴ γῆ
καὶ στὴ φυγὴ δὲν ἄπλωσα τὰ μυστικὰ φτερά μου,
μὰ ὁλάκερον ἐρίζωσα τὸ νοῦ μου στὴ σιγή,
νά ποὺ καὶ πάλι ἀναπηδᾶ στὴ δίψα μου ἡ πηγή,
πηγὴ ζωῆς, χορευτικὴ πηγή, πηγὴ χαρά μου...

Γιατὶ ποτὲ δὲ λόγιασα τὸ πότε καὶ τὸ πῶς,
μὰ ἐβύθισα τὴ σκέψη μου μέσα στὴν πᾶσαν ὥρα,
σὰ μέσα της νὰ κρύβονταν ὁ ἀμέτρητος σκοπός,
νά τώρα πού, ἢ καλοκαιριὰ τριγύρα μου εἴτε μπόρα,
λάμπ' ἡ στιγμὴ ὁλοστρόγγυλη στὸ νοῦ μου σὰν ὀπώρα,
βρέχει ἀπ' τὰ βάθη τ' οὐρανοῦ καὶ μέσα μου ὁ καρπός!...

Γιατὶ δὲν εἶπα: «ἐδῶ ἡ ζωὴ ἀρχίζει, ἐδῶ τελειώνει...»
μὰ «ἂν εἶν' ἡ μέρα βροχερή, σέρνει πιὸ πλούσιο φῶς...
μὰ κι ὁ σεισμὸς βαθύτερη τὴ χτίση θεμελιώνει,
τὶ ὁ ζωντανὸς παλμὸς τῆς γῆς ποὺ πλάθει εἶναι κρυφός...»
νά πού, ὅ,τι στάθη ἐφήμερο, σὰ σύγνεφο ἀναλιώνει,
νά ποὺ κι ὁ μέγας Θάνατος μοῦ γίνηκε ἀδερφός!...

42

BECAUSE I DEEPLY PRAISED

Because I deeply praised and trusted earth
and did not spread my secret wings in flight
but rooted in the stillness all my mind,
the spring again has risen to my thirst,
the dancing spring of life, my own joy's spring.

Because I never questioned how and when
but plunged my thought into each passing hour
as though its boundless goal lay hidden there,
no matter if I live in calm or storm,
the rounded moment shimmers in my mind,
the fruit falls from the sky, falls deep inside me.

Because I did not say: "here life starts, here ends,"
but "days of rain bring on a richer light
and earthquakes give the world a firmer base,
for secret is earth's live creative pulse,"
all fleeting things dissolve away like clouds,
great Death itself has now become my kin.

43

Ο ΧΩΡΙΑΤΙΚΟΣ ΓΑΜΟΣ

Σταματημένα τ' ἄλογα
ἃς προσμένουν στὴν πλακόστρωτη ἁπλωσιὰ
π' ὅλη γεμίζει ἀπὸ τὸ χτύπο τοῦ πετάλου
ὅπως πληθαίνει τὸ συμπεθεριό·

καὶ στριμωγμένες ξαφνικά,
καπούλια μὲ καπούλια οἱ μοῦλες
ἃς σηκώνονται στὰ πισινὰ γι' ἀπλοχωριά·

κι ὅλη ἃς γιομίζει ποδοβολητό, χλιμίντρισμα,
ἡ αὐλή·

ἐνῶ στὶς ράχες τους
στρωμένες μὲ σκουρόχρωμα φαντά,
μὲ τὸ πλευρὸ καβάλα οἱ συμπεθέρες,
στολισμένες σὲ μετάξια καὶ χρυσά,
τινάζουνε ἀπαλὰ τὰ γκέμια
νὰ κινήσουνε μαζὶ
(κ' εἶναι ἡ γαλάζια μέρα, ἡ Κυριακή,
κι ἀπὸ τὰ βάθη τοῦ χωριοῦ
τῆς νιᾶς καμπάνας χύνεται ἡ βοὴ
σὰ μιᾶς γελάδας
ποὺ ἀγκουσεύει τὸ περίσσιο γάλα
τὸ πονετικὸ μουκανητό·

κι ὅλο ἔχ' ἀδειάσει τὸ χωριὸ
στὸ λιόχαρον ἀλώνι
ὀμπρὸς στὴν ἐκκλησιά!)

THE VILLAGE WEDDING*

Let the tethered horses
wait on the cobblestones
which echo with the clatter of horseshoes
as the bridegroom's party gathers;

and let the mules, suddenly crowded
croup to croup,
rise on their hind legs for room;

and let the whole courtyard
fill with hoofbeats, with neighing;

while on their backs
spread with dark woven cloth
the bridegroom and his party
riding sidesaddle,
adorned with silk and gold,
gently shake the reins
to move off together
(and it is a fine blue day, Sunday,
and from the heart of the village
the sound of the new bell spills
like a cow's plaintive call
when her udders
are swollen with too much milk;

and the whole village has emptied
onto the sunlit threshing-floor
in front of the church).

45

Μὰ στὸ χωριὸ τ' ἀντικρινὸ
ὅλο ἂς πληθαίνει ἡ διάφανη σιωπή!

Στημένη ἡ νύφη
σὲ θρονὶ ποὺ ἀστράφτει, χαμηλό,

μήτε δεξὰ ἂς κοιτάει μήτε ζερβά,
ἐνῶ οἱ στολίστρες
πίσω ἀπὸ τοὺς ὤμους της ὀρτὲς
ἀπ' τὴν κορφὴ τοῦ κεφαλιοῦ της
τῆς χωρίζουνε στὴ μέση τὰ μαλλιά,
κι ἀφοῦ τὰ στρώσουν μὲ τὸ χτένι
καὶ στὸν ἀέρα τὰ τινάξουν δῶθε κεῖθε
δυνατά,
στὰ τρία τους δάχτυλα χωρίζοντας
τὸν ἁπαλόνε θησαυρό,

μὲ ἥσυχα χέρια ἀρχίζουνε
νὰ δένουν τὶς πλεξοῦδες
σὰ σφεντόνα
ἀπανωτά!

(Στὸ μεσοδόκι τοῦ σπιτιοῦ
ἡ πνοὴ τ' ἀγέρα ἀπὸ τὴ θύρα,
στὴ γαλάζια σκιά,
ἂς λούζει ὡστόσο τ' ἀνεμόχορτο
ποὺ πιάνει ἡ ρίζα του στὸν ἀέρα τοῦ βουνοῦ,

ἢ τὸ ξερὸ χελιδονόψαρο
μὲ τεντωτὲς φτεροῦγες,
στοῦ θαλασσινοῦ τὸ σπίτι
ζυγιασμένο ἀπὸ ψηλά,

46

But in the village opposite
let the diaphanous silence grow.

The bride sits
on a low polished stool,

she looks neither right nor left
as the bridesmaids,
standing behind her back,
part her hair in the middle
along the crown of her head,
and when they have combed it through,
shaken it out into the air,
powerfully,
with three fingers separating
the soft treasure,

their quiet hands begin
to braid the plaits
like slings
one on top of the other.
(Let the breeze from the door
bathe the basil-leaved herb
that grows in the mountain air
as it hangs in the blue shade
from the great beam of the house,

or the dry flying-fish,
its wings outspread,
balanced high
in this sailor's home,

στὸ ἀγέρι ποὺ φυσᾷ κάθε φορὰ
δοσμένο,
ὡς τὸ καΐκι τοῦ ξενιτεμένου νοικοκύρη
στὴν πνοὴ τοῦ Θεοῦ!

Στοὺς ἄσπρους τοίχους
τὰ πλεγμένα στάχυα ἃς λάμπουν καρφωτά,

κι ἀπ' τό 'να στ' ἄλλο παραθύρι
ἃς σαϊτεύει ἀστράφτοντας
ἡ γληγοράδα τοῦ χελιδονιοῦ!

Μὰ ἀπὸ τὴ νύφη, ἀσάλευτη, τριγύρα,
σκεπασμένη τώρα στ' ἀραχνόφαντο κεφαλοπάνι,
ἃς ξεχειλίζει ἡ διάφανη σιγή,

κι ὁ ἀπάρθενος ἃς ρεύει λογισμός,
καθὼς στὰ πλάγια τὰ βαθύχλοα
στὸν ἀπάνεμο ἥλιο
τ' ἀνθορρόημα μιᾶς ἀγραπιδᾶς.)

Μέσα στὸν πέπλο σου ἄκουσες,
βουβή, θεοσάλευτη καρδιά;

Νά το τὸ πρῶτο πάτημα τῶν μουλαριῶν
ποὺ ἀνακυκλᾶνε τὰ λιθάρια χαμηλά!

Μὰ στὸ ἄτι ἀπάνου, πόρχεται μπροστά, ὁ γαμπρὸς
τὴν πλάσην ὅλη χαίρεται προικιό!

48

exposed to every wind that blows,
like the caique
of the bride's seafaring father
to the breath of God.

Nailed to the white walls
let the interwoven wheatears gleam,

and from the one window to the other
let the swallow fly
quick as lightning.

But around the bride, motionless,
covered now with the delicate headdress,
let the crystal silence pour,

and let her virginal thought flow
as on grassy slopes,
in the windless sun,
the wild pear tree unfolds its flowers.)

Do you listen within your veil,
silent, God-quickened heart?

There it is, the first tread of the mules
scattering the stones as they come.

But riding a stallion, leading the way, the bridegroom
greets all creation as his dowry.

49

Πίνει τὸν ἥλιο τὸ κορμί του,
πίνει ὡς μιὰ ζεστὴ ψιλὴ ἀμμουδιὰ
τὸν πάντα νέον ἀφρό!

Κόκκινο φλάμπουρον ἀλύγιστο
βαρὺ ἀπὸ κέντημα σγουρὸ κι ἀνεβατό,
μὲ κρόσσια ὡσὰ βαριὰ βαλάνια, ἀρίθμητα, χρυσά,
πετάει φουχτιὲς ἀχτίδες
μπρὸς στὰ μάτια του
ἡ καρδιά!

Κι ἀκούει!

Ἀκούει τὴν κίσσα
ποὺ ἀπ' τῆς λεύκας τὴν κορφὴ
πέφτει σὲ ἀμπέλι
μὲ μιὰ λιόχαρη φωνή·

ἀκούει τὰ σκόρπια τὰ βελάσματα μακριά·
βλέπει μὲ τ' ἄσπρο τοῦ ματιοῦ
τὸν ἴσκιο τῆς σβιλάδας στὰ σπαρτά!

Σφιχτοπατάει τὶς σκάλες τοῦ φαριοῦ
ὡς τοῦ χορεύει δυνατὰ ἡ πνοή.

Ἡ δύναμή του ὀργώνεται καὶ κλεῖ
καθὼς τὸ χῶμα πίσω ἀπ' τὸ γενί!

50

His body drinks the sun,
drinks as a hot beach of fine sand
the ever-renewing foam.

Red unyielding banner,
heavy with thick dark embroidery,
with tassels, golden, numberless, like thick acorns,
his heart
discharges fistfuls of light
in front of his eyes.

And he listens.

He hears the ivy
that from the tip of the poplar
falls into a vineyard
with a small happy cry;

he hears in the distance the sporadic bleat of sheep;
he sees from the corner of his eye
the gust's shadow in the field of wheat.

He spurs his horse
until its breath dances strongly.

His strength is tilled, it closes
like soil behind the ploughshare.

51

Καὶ τέλος νά·
σὰν ξεπεζεύει στὸ κατώφλι τοῦ σπιτιοῦ.
στὸ ἀντίκρισμα τῆς νύφης
τοῦ σωπαίνει ξαφνικὰ ἡ καρδιά!

(Ὢ βάθος καὶ σιωπὴ τῆς Παρθενιᾶς!)

Σὰ συγνεφιὰ ἀνοιξιάτικη ἂς ἁπλώσει τώρα
τὸ στεφανοσκέπασμα, γλυκά.

Σὰν ἡ ψιχάλα ἡ ἀνοιξιάτικη
τὸ ρίζι τὸ κάτασπρο ἂς τιναχτεῖ!

Στὸ φῶς τῆς μέρας
ἂς ψηλώνει ἀχνόχρυση ὁλοένα
στὰ γυμνὰ φιτίλια
ἡ φλόγα τῶν κεριῶν!

Καὶ τώρα πιὰ
διαβαίνει ἡ περιστέρα
γιὰ τὸ σπίτι τοῦ γαμπροῦ.

Μὰ ἡ μάνα ἐκεῖ
στὴ θύρα ὀμπρὸς
τοὺς σταματᾶ.

Κι ἀκούγετ' ἡ ἄφθαρτη φωνή:

52

And at last
dismounting at the threshold of the house,
facing the bride,
his heart suddenly stills.

(O depth and stillness of Virginity!)

Like a spring cloud let the bridal wreaths
gently crown their heads.

Let the white rice be thrown
like a spring shower.

In the light of day
let the flames of the candles
like fine gold
rise from their naked wicks.

And now at last the pigeon
takes wing
for the bridegroom's house.

But the bride's mother,
standing at the door,
stops them.

And her deathless voice is heard:

53

«Στοῦ κατωφλιοῦ τὴν πλάκα
κι ἂν τὸ γράψεις, θυγατέρα,
δὲ στέκει τ᾽ ὄνομά σου.
Πέρνα καθὼς περνάει τὸ χελιδόνι.
Κι ἂν θὲς νὰ μὴ σταθεῖς, μὴ ἰδεῖς μπροστά σου·
διάβα καθὼς μὲ τὸ βαρὺ λαγήνι
τὸ γεμάτο νερό, ποὺ μὲ μονάχα
τὸ κεφάλι τὸ ἀνέβαζες στὸ σπίτι
καὶ δὲν ἐκοίταζες μπροστά, οὔτε πίσω
— δεξά, ζερβὰ δὲν κοίταζες — καὶ μήτε
τὰ χέρια γύρα σου ἔψαχναν ὁλοένα
μὰ ἔστριβαν τὸ μαλλὶ κ᾽ ἦταν πιασμένα·
τὸ κατώφλι ἔτσι πέρνα, θυγατέρα!

» Κ᾽ ἐκεῖ, γαμπρέ, πόχει ὁ λαιμὸς χαράκι
σὰν ἡ τρυγόνα κι ὡς ἡ περιστέρα,
ἐκεῖ μονάχα ἐγράφτη τὸ σημάδι
(κι ὡς τότε ἀπάνω της μὴ βάλεις χέρι)
τὸ κορμὶ νὰ χωρίσει ἀπ᾽ τὸ κεφάλι,
τῆς ἀπιστιᾶς ἂν ξημερώσει ἡ μέρα!

» Θυγατέρα, σὰν ἔβγεις παρακάτου,
στοῦ πηγαδιοῦ θ᾽ ἀνέβεις τὸ ζωνάρι
νὰ πιεῖς στερνὸ ἀπ᾽ τὸ χέρι μου ποτήρι
νὰ χαιρετήσεις τὰ νερὰ τοῦ τόπου.
Θὰ πιεῖς νερὸ ὅσο ζητᾶ ἡ καρδιά σου,
κι ὅσο μείνει, τῆς μάνας σου θὰ μείνει,
π᾽ ἄδειασ᾽ ὅλ᾽ ἡ καρδιά της ἀπ᾽ τό κλάμα.

"Your name, daughter,
won't stay on the stone slab of the threshold
even if you write it there.
Pass as the swallow passes;
if you don't want to falter
don't stop to look in front of you,
go as you did when you carried,
simply, on your head,
a pitcher full of water into the house,
looking neither right nor left,
neither in front nor behind, your hands
not searching around you at all
but twisting wool into thread, occupied:
cross the threshold like that, daughter.

And, bridegroom, there where her throat is ringed
like the dove's or the pigeon's,
there alone let the mark be cut
for her head to be severed from her body
should the day of unfaithfulness dawn—
and before that day lay no harsh hand on her.

Daughter, when you depart,
you will go up to the well,
to drink the last cup from my hand,
to say goodbye to the water of this village.
You will drink as your heart desires,
and what is left will be for your mother
who empties her whole heart with her tears.

» Θυγατέρα, στὸ σπίτι ὅπου πηγαίνεις,
ἀπὸ μιὰ θύρα ὡς θὰ διαβαίνεις σ' ἄλλη,
νὰ μὴν ἀκούγεται τὸ πάτημά σου!
Σὰν τὸ σπιτόφιδο ἂς γενεῖ ἡ καρδιά σου!
Σὰ ζυγαριὰ μπροστὰ ἀπ' τὸν ἄντρα στάσου!

» Τὸν ὕπνο κράτει καθαρὸ θεμέλιο,
στὶς τέσσερις γωνιὲς ἡ δύναμή σου
νὰ φέγγει τοῦ σπιτιοῦ, καὶ τὰ ὄνειρά σου
νὰ λὲν τὴ μέρα, ὄρθρο βαθύ, δική σου.

» Πέρνα, ἡ θύρα εἶν' ἐλεύτερη μπροστά σου . . . »

Σάν ἄσπρη τρεχαντήρα νιά,
ὁποὺ ὅλο τὸ θαλασσοχώρι, σπρώχνοντας
τὴν κατεβάζει στὸ γιαλό,
τραβάει μαζὶ τὴ νύφη τὸ συμπεθεριό.

Στὸ δυνατὸ κατήφορο
τὰ νιοκαλλίγωτα ἄλογα γλιστρᾶν.

Στὸ διάβα
ἀπ' τὰ κατώφλια πίσω,

σὲ ραβδιὰ οἱ γριὲς ἀκουμπισμένες
ἥσυχα κοιτᾶν.

Καὶ νά τὸ νιὸ τὸ σπίτι ἀπὸ μακριά!

56

Daughter, don't let your step be heard
as you cross from one door to the other
in the house to which you are going.
Let your heart become like the house-snake.
Stand before your husband like a balanced scale.

Hold sleep as a pure foundation,
so that your strength
radiates to the four corners of the house,
and your dreams
announce, at early dawn, that the day is your own.

Go, the door is open in front of you. . ."

Like a new white fishing boat
that the whole fishing village
pushes down to the shore,
the bridegroom's party draws the bride after them.

On the steep slope
the freshly shod horses slip.

From behind their thresholds
the old women,

leaning on their sticks,
gaze calmly at the passing procession.

And there in the distance is the new home.

Μὲ μέλι ἀλείβει τὸ κατώφλι
ἡ μάνα τοῦ γαμπροῦ,

στ' ἀνώφλι σπάει τὸ ρόιδι
πρὶν ἡ νύφη προσδιαβεῖ.

Τὸ τυλιγμένο στρῶμα ἀνοίγοντας
ἃς πλημμυρίσει τώρα ὅλο τὸ θάλαμο καρπούς!

Ὁ πέπλος κάτου ἃς τιναχτεῖ
καθὼς ὁ ἀνθὸς μιᾶς μυγδαλιᾶς!

Σὰν ἀπὸ μάρμαρο ἃς φαντάζει ἡ κλίνη
στὶς ψυχὲς τῶν νιόγαμπρων μπροστά!

Ὦ κρύα φαντὰ σεντόνια
ὡς χιόνια τοῦ Μαρτιοῦ!

Ὦ φρένα θαμπωμένα μπρὸς στὸ διάπλατο βωμό!

Ὦ σάρκα παγωμένη ὥσμε τὰ νύχια, στὴν ἀρχή!

Ἀναπνοὴ
σὰν κρίνου, ποὺ κρουστάλλιασε ὁ βοριάς!

Πορτοκαλάνθια
κρεμασμένα σὲ θανάτου ἀπάρθενου τ' ὁλάσπρο φῶς!

Ὦ, σὰν τὰ φίδια ἀπ' τὸ χειμώνα
μέσ' ἀπ' τὸ γλυκό σου λήθαργο ξυπνώντας,
Παρθενιά!

58

Before the bride enters,
the bridegroom's mother

annoints the threshold with honey,
breaks the pomegranate on the lintel.

As the rolled mattress opens
let the whole bridal chamber smell of fruit.

Let the bride throw off her veil
as an almond tree casts its blossom.

Let the bed seem of marble
to the souls of the bridal couple.

O cool woven sheets
like the snows of March.

O mind dazzled before the open altar.

Flesh chilled at first to the fingertips.

Breath
like a lily that the north wind has frozen.

Orange-blossom
hung in the white light of a virginal death.

As snakes from winter
you wake from your sweet drowsiness,
Virginity.

Καὶ ξαφνικὰ
στῆς προσμονῆς τὸ βάθος,
ὦ κερήθρας μυρουδιά!

Ὦ ξάφνου μὲς στὸν οὐρανίσκο ἀπιθωμένη
ἀνάπνοια τοῦ μελιοῦ!

Ἀγέρα, ξαφνικὰ παραμερίζοντας
σὰν ἄσπρος πέπλος,
ἀπ' τὸ γόνα τοῦ γαμπροῦ!

Πλάση τοῦ ἀντρὸς ἀπ' τὴν ἀρχὴ
στὸ Λόγο τὸ θεϊκό!

Ἀπ' τὸ πλευρό του μυστικὰ θρεμμένη
ὁλόσωμη χαρά!

Τώρα τὰ χέρια, στὰ λυτὰ μαλλιὰ χωμένα,
ἂς τὰ βυθίζει ἀκέρια
ὡς σὲ σωρὸ σταριοῦ!

Τώρα ἂς θερίσει τὸν κατάβαθον ἀγρὸ
τῆς πλάστρας μυρωδιᾶς!

Ἡ μυριανάπνοη ὥρα ἂς στυλωθεῖ!

Μὲς στὴν καρδιά, πρωτόλουβο τὸ γέλιο,
ὅλο σκιρτώντας σὰν τὰ πρῶτα κύματα
ἀπὸ τὸν ἀγέρα πόρχεται μακριάθε
στὰ πετράδια τῆς ἀκρογιαλιᾶς,

And suddenly,
from the depths of their expectation,
the scent of the hive.

O sudden breath of honey
on the palate.

Breeze suddenly brushing
the bridegroom's knee
like a white veil.

Creation of man from the beginning
at the Word of God.

From his side full-bodied joy
mysteriously nourished.

Let him now plunge his hands wholly
into her loosened hair
as into a heap of wheat.

Let him now reap the deepest field
of creative fragrance.

Let the hour of countless breaths be strengthened.

In his heart let the first ripening laugh,
leaping like the first waves
on the pebbles of the beach
when the wind comes from far away,

61

ἂς ἁπλωθεῖ κρυφὴ ἁρμονία
ὅλο σαλεύοντας τὸ νοῦ!

῎Ας σκάσει μέσα στὴν ψυχή του
ἀπὸ τὴν πύρη τῆς χαρᾶς
καθὼς ἡ δάφνη καὶ τ' ἀλάτι στὴ φωτιά!

Κι ὤ, νιὰ γαλήνη τῆς νυφιάτικης αὐγῆς!

Πιθώνοντας τὸ πόδι κάτου,
ἀνοίγει πιὰ τὴ θύρα βγαίνοντας σὲ ναό!

Στὸν ἴσκιο τῆς χαρᾶς του
ὡς κάτου ἀπό 'να πλάτανο
ἂς τρώει κι ἂς πίνει κι ἂς χορεύει τὸ χωριό!

Καὶ μπρὸς ἀπὸ τὴ νύφη,
ὡς ἀπὸ βρύση κρούσταλλου νεροῦ,
ἂς προσπερνᾶνε οἱ φιλενάδες
συντηρώντας τὴν εἰδή της μὲ τὴν ἄκρη τοῦ ματιοῦ
σὰ νὰ ζυγιάζαν στὸ κεφάλι τὰ σταμνιά!

῎Ω, ποὺ ἀκλουθᾶς τὸν ἄντρα
ὅπως ξοπίσω ἀπ' τὸ σταφύλι
ἀκολουθάει τ' ἀρνί!

Δεμένη παρθενιά,
ποὺ ὁ πόθος,
σὰ μιὰ τρίαινα μπήγοντας τὰ δόντια της στὸ βράχο,
ξεχειλίζει τὸ βαθιό σου γέλιο
ὡς κρεμαστὴ πηγή!

62

spread its secret harmony,
moving the whole mind.

Let it break in his soul
from the fire of joy
like laurel and salt in the flames.

And oh, the peace of the bridal dawn!

Rising at last
he opens the door and enters
the temple of wonder around him.

In the shadow of his joy
as under a plane tree
let the village eat, drink, and dance.

And as in front of a fount of crystal water
let the girls
pass in front of the bride
observing her look from the corner of their eyes
as though balancing pitchers on their heads.

O you who follow your man
as the lamb
follows behind the grape,

pledged virginity
whose longing
—like a harpoon piercing the rock with its barbs—
issues like a cascade
in your deep laughter.

Ὢ, ποὖ, ὅπως ἡ Λητὼ γεννώντας τὸν Ἀπόλλωνα
ἐκράτει ὀρτὴ στὴ Δῆλο τὴν αἰθέρια φοινικιά,
μὲ χέρια ἀχνὰ κι ἀνάλαφρα
πιασμένη ἀπ' τ' ἄντρα τὴ γερὴ καρδιὰ
φέρνεις στὸν κόσμο
— εἰκόνα μυστική της —
τὸ παιδί,
μὲ μιὰ κραυγή σου,
καθὼς τὸ ἔργο
ὁ Ποιητής!

Oh, like Leto giving birth to Apollo
when, standing, her hands slight and pale,
she clasped the ethereal palm tree on Delos,
may you—her mystical image—
held by your husband's strong heart,
bring into the world
with a single cry
your child
as the Poet brings forth
his creation.

ΥΜΝΟΣ ΣΤΗΝ ΟΡΘΙΑ ΑΡΤΕΜΙΔΑ

Ὠ Ταΰγετε,
χαλκὸ βουνό,
ὡς μὲ δέχτης τέλος ἀσκητή!

Ὠ σκισμένα ὄρη,
ὅταν ἐκλείσατε ἀπὸ πίσω μου
ἀφήνοντάς με ὁλόμονο,
ὅπως σὰν ἕνα κριάρι κατεβεῖ
ἀπ᾽ ὀρτὴ πλαγιὰ σ᾽ ἕνα πετρόλακκο
καὶ ξαφνικὰ γυρίζοντας νὰ φύγει
νιώθει πὼς δὲν εἶναι δυνατὸ

γιατ᾽ οἱ ἴδιοι βράχοι
ποὺ τὸ βοήθησαν νὰ κατεβεῖ
τώρα γλιστρᾶνε στὸ ἀνηφόρι
ἀπάτητοι
παντοῦ!

Ὁλόμονο μὲ κλείσατε
μὲς στὴν ἀκρότατη ἐρημιά,
μονάχα νὰ σαλεύω ὁλόγυρα στὴ φτέρνα μου,
νὰ σὲ κοιτάζω, κάστρο ἀτέλειωτο χαλκό!

Οὔτε μπροστά, οὔτε πίσω!
ἀλλὰ κεῖ, στὸν ἴδιο τόπο ἀπάνου
δίχως σπιθαμὴ τριγύρα ν᾽ ἀκουμπήσω ἢ ν᾽ ἁπλωθῶ,
ἀλλὰ κεῖ, στὸν ἴδιο πάντα τόπο
ὀρτός!

HYMN TO ARTEMIS ORTHIA *

O Taygetus,
bronze mountain,
at last you receive me as an ascetic!

Jagged range,
you closed behind me,
leaving me in solitude
as when a ram descends
down a steep cliff into a rocky cleft
and, suddenly turning,
realizes that he cannot go back,

because the same rocks
that helped him to descend
now slip as he climbs up,
slip on every side,
offering no foothold.

In solitude you enclosed me,
in the extreme wilderness,
able only to pivot on my own heel,
to gaze at you, huge bronze fortress!

Neither forward nor back,
but here, on this spot,
without room to lie down or stretch out,
here on this same spot,
upright.

67

Ὦ πυροδότη τῶν ἀνθρώπων,
δὲν ἄκουα ν' ἀνεβαίνει κάτουθε,
ἀπὸ τὸν τραχὺ γκρεμό,
ἡ παρηγοριὰ τῶν 'Ωκεανίδων !

ἀλλ' ἀπ' ὁλοῦθε ὁ βράχος
ἡ καρδιὰ τῆς γῆς
τὸ χῶμα ποὺ κάθ' ὥρα ἀνάδινε
μιὰ μυρωδιὰ ψηλότερη ἀπὸ πελαγίσια τρικυμιά,
βουλιάζοντας καὶ παίζοντας στὰ κύματά της
ἄπλερο ἕνα σκάφος
τὴ μικρή μου ἀναπνοή !

Κι ὅλο μου τὸ αἷμα ἦταν βοὴ στ' αὐτιά μου
καὶ στὰ μάτια μου μιὰ ἀνάβρα σπίθες,
ὅπως ἡ πρωτάναφτη φωτιὰ μὲς στὸ καμίνι
ὀμπρὸς στὸ φυσερό !

'Αλλ' ὅταν τέλος ἀπιθώθηκε ἡ ψυχή μου
στὴν ἀδάμαστή σου, Ταΰγετε, εὐωδιά,

κ' ἡ θλιβερὴ καρδιά μου
ποὺ ἐθρηνοῦσε στὴ νυχτιὰ
καθὼς ὁ γκιώνης
ποὺ κρέμεται ἀνάποδα τὴ νύχτα ἀπ' τὸ κλαδὶ
ἀφήνοντας τὸ θρῆνο νὰ σταλάζει
ὁλόζεστος στὴ γῆ,

O you who gave fire to man,*
I have not heard
from the foot of the precipice
the consolation of the Oceanides.

But on all sides the rock,
the heart of earth,
the soil that at each moment gave out
a smell more pungent than that of a sea storm,
sinking and playing among its waves
like a young ship:
my puny breath!

And my blood throbbed in my ears,
and my eyes sparkled
like a new-lit fire in the grate
fanned by the bellows.

But, Taygetus, when at last my soul
rested on your wild fragrance,

and my afflicted heart—
lamenting throughout the night
like the Scops owl
that hangs upside down from the branch
letting its lament drip,
still warm, into the earth,

69

κι ὡς τὸ σφαγμένο ἀρνὶ
ποὺ τὸ κρεμᾶν μὲ τὸ κεφάλι κάτου
γιὰ νὰ τρέξει τὸ περίσσιον αἶμα ἀπὸ τὸ στόμα,

νιώστη ξάφνου ὡς μὲς σ' ἀιτοφωλιὰ
ποὺ εἶν' ὅλη καμωμένη ἀπὸ ξερὰ κλαδιὰ
φτωχὴ καὶ στέρεη σὰ μιὰ πυροστιά,

ὦ νέες πνοὲς
ποὺ ἐθρέψατε τὴ δύναμή μου ἀδάμαστη καὶ σιωπηλή,

πέπλε τῆς βοῆς στὶς πέντε σου βουνοκορφὲς
ποὺ σιγολιώνανε τὰ χιόνια,

ἀνάεροι καταρράχτες
τῆς μπουμπουκιασμένης ῥοδοδάφνης
στὰ γκρεμνά,

ἀνατολὴ τοῦ Δώριου Ἀπόλλωνα
στὰ μάτια μου μπροστά,
ὦ ὄψη σκληρὴ καὶ σκαλιστὴ
στὸν κόκκινον ἀμάλαγο χαλκό!

ὦ μάτια μου, θρεμμένα τέλος
σὰν τοῦ λιονταριοῦ
μὲς στὸ ἄπαρτο σκοτάδι τοῦ βουνοῦ!

σιωπὴ βαθιὰ
ποὺ δὲν ἐσάλευε μιὰ πνοή,
καὶ τὰ ἴδια χέρια μου ἦταν ἄφαντα
στὴν πίσσα τῆς βουβῆς βραδιᾶς,

70

and like the slaughtered lamb
that they hang head down
so that the excess blood can run from its mouth—

when my afflicted heart suddenly felt itself
in an eagle's nest made of dry twigs,
simple and firm like a trivet,

what new impulses
nourished my untamable and silent strength,

veil of the tumult on your five peaks
where the snow was slowly thawing,

aerial cataracts
of the flowering oleander
on the escarpments,

dawning of the Doric Apollo
before my eyes,
O harsh sculptured form
on the red unsoftened bronze!

My eyes, fed at last like the lion's
in the impenetrable dark of the mountain!

deep silence,
where no breath stirs,
and my hands invisible
in the pitch-black, the voiceless night,

71

ὦ στοχασμοί,
σὰ νυχτερίδες κυκλοφέρνοντας στὴ σκιά,

σὰν ἄξαφνα ἀπ' τὴ Σπάρτη
ἐπρόβαλε κατάνακρα
τεράστια κι ὁλοστρόγγυλη
βαμμένη στὸ αἷμα,
Ὀρθία Ἀρτέμιδα,
ὡς ἀσπίδα Σου
ἡ Πανσέληνο,
κ' Ἐσύ, ἀπὸ πίσω,
πιότερο ἀπὸ νύχτα
ἀλύγιστη κι ἀμίλητη καὶ σκοτεινή!

Τὰ πρῶτα βέλη Σου
ἄρχισαν δονώντας τὴ σιγή!

Γύρω ἀπ' τ' αὐτιά μου ἐσούριζαν
ἀνάρια σταφνισμένα
ὡς σὲ σημάδι μὲς στὰ σκότη
ὅπου Σὺ μόνον ἔβλεπες ψηλά!

Λαμπρίζαν χαμηλὰ στρωμένα
τὰ πλεχτὰ καλάμια
ἀπ' τὴ δροσιὰ τοῦ Εὐρώτα.

thoughts
like bats circling in the shadow,

when suddenly from Sparta
the full moon
rose before me
huge, round,
dipped in blood
like Your shield, Artemis Orthia,
with You Yourself behind it,
inexorable, silent,
darker than night.

Your first arrows
began to shatter the silence.

They whistled around my ears
aimed one by one
as though at a target in the dark
that only You, from on high, could see.

The interwoven reeds
spread out below
shone with the dews of the Eurotas.

Στὴν κόκκινη πεδιάδα
οὔρλιασαν τότε οἱ Λάκαινες οἱ σκύλες
μὲ τὴν τρίχα ὀρτήν, ἀκούοντας ἀπὸ πάνω τους
τὸ μήνυμα τοῦ τόξου Σου,
καὶ τρίζανε τὰ δόντια τους
κατάματα κοιτάζοντας τὸ τέρας τῆς Σελήνης
πὄκρυβε τὸ σιωπηλό Σου ἀγώνα
ὡς πίσω ἀπὸ φωτιά!

Ἕτοιμος γιὰ τὸ θάνατον,
ἀφεύγατο ὡς τὸν ἔνιωθα ἀπὸ Σέ,
σηκώθηκα στὰ νύχια
καὶ στυλώνοντάς Σέ,

ὅπως Ἐσὺ
ποὺ ἐξέσερνες τὸ βέλος ὣς τ᾽ αὐτί Σου
γιὰ νὰ ξέρεις, ἀπ᾽ τὸν ἦχο
π᾽ ἄφηνε στὸ ἀπόλυμα ἡ νευρή,
ἂν λάθειψεν ἢ ἐβρῆκε τὸ σκοπό.

ἔτσι ἔφερα στ᾽ αὐτί μου
ἕνα πρὸς ἕνα
κάθε λόγο,
πρὶν τὸ στόμα μου,
ποὺ κλειδωμένο τό ᾽φραζαν τὰ δόντια ὡσὰ νεκροῦ,

ἀνοίξει στὸ βαρύτερο Ὕμνο
ποὺ ζυγιάστηκε στὸν Ἔρωτα τῆς Γῆς,

στὸ χῶμα τῆς καρδιᾶς καὶ τοῦ θανάτου μου,

74

Then in the red plain
the Laconian bitches howled,
their hair on end
as they heard above them
the message of Your bow,
and they gnashed their teeth
staring at the prodigious moon
that hid Your silent struggle
as though behind fire.

Prepared for death,
steadfast until I felt it from You,
I stood on tiptoe,
my attention fixed on You,

and as You
drew the arrow back to Your ear
to learn from the string's vibration
whether it had found or missed its mark,

so I brought to my ear
each word
one by one,
before my mouth—
closed until then,
teeth clenched like a dead man's—

opened in a more solemn Hymn
that plumbed to the Eros of Earth,

to the soil of my heart and my death:

75

ʼΟρθία, σʼ Ἐσέ!

«Ὢ ποὺ σκυμμένη ὡς ψάχνεις
τὰ σαγόνια τῶν λαγωνικῶν Σου,
ὅλα μαζί
στὸ πρῶτο τάνυσμα τοῦ τόξου
λαχανιάζοντας γιὰ νὰ Σὲ φτάσουν
ἅμα ὁρμήσεις στὸ κυνήγι
προσδιαβαίνουν τὸ σκοπό,
κι ὅπου σταθεῖς
ὅλα μαζὶ
κρεμώντας στὸ λαχάνιασμα τὴ γλώσσα
ζώνοντάς Σε μὲ χαρὲς
σκορπᾶν στὴν ὄψη Σου τὸ χνῶτο τους καυτό!

» Ὢ ʼΟρθία·
ποὺ στὸ τυφλὸ σκοτάδι
τὸ σκληρὸν ἀσπράδι τῆς ματιᾶς Σου
ἀστράφτει ὡσὰν τὰ δόντια τοῦ βουνόλυκου
ποὺ μὲ τὰ χείλια ἀνασκωμένα
ρυάζεται γιὰ νὰ χυθεῖ!

» Μὲ ποιὰ κραυγὴ
στρέφεις τὰ πάντα
στὴν ἐπιθυμιά τους καὶ τὴ δύναμή τους
ξαφνικά!

76

a Hymn, Orthia, to You.

"O You who bend down to feel
the muzzles of Your hounds
that at the first stretching of the bow
all rush forward with You
and overshoot the target
as You lead the chase,
and when You halt
they all halt,
breathlessly lolling their tongues,
circling You in their joy
and spattering Your face with their hot breath.

O Orthia,
in the blind darkness
the harsh white of Your eye
flashes like the wolf's teeth
when, with lips snarling,
he howls as he gathers himself to spring.

How Your cry
suddenly turns all things
to the source of their desire and their strength.

» Καὶ νά·
ἡ βουκέντρα, τ' ἄτια, τὰ σκυλιὰ
τὸ χῶμα, τὰ νερὰ
κάτου ἀπ' τὴν ἴδια ὁρμὴ καὶ δίψα Σου
ἀκλουθᾶν!

» Στέρεο σκαλί Σου ὁ θάνατος
γιὰ ν' ἀνεβεῖς!

» Πλεχτὴ σφεντόνα ἡ κόμη Σου,
καὶ τὸ θηλύκι τὸ ἀτσαλένιο τοῦ βυζιοῦ Σου
ἀμάλαγο καὶ σκοτεινό!

» Δὲν ἔσκυψες νὰ ὀργώσεις μὲ γενὶ τὴ γῆν
ἀλλὰ ἐμαστίγωσες ὡς τὸ αἷμα
τοὺς ἐφήβους σιωπηλή,

» κι ἀπάνω τους σκυμμένη ἡ παρθενιά Σου,
ποὺ ἱδρωμένη ἐμυροβόλα
πιότερο ἀπ' τοῦ δάσου τὴν καρδιά,
τοὺς κέντριζε
ὥσμε τὴ στερνὴν ἀνάπνοια
στὴν ἀνηφοριά,

» στὸ στεγνωμένο τους λαρύγγι τάζοντας
πηγὴ μονάχη
τὴν κορφή!

78

And all things—
whip, dogs, horses,
soil, waters—
follow
in the wake of Your onrush and thirst.

Death is a firm ladder
for You to climb up.

Your hair is a woven sling,
and Your steel nipples
are unsoftened and dark.

You did not stoop to sow the earth with wheat,
but in silence You whipped
the young men until they bled,

and Your own virginal figure bending over them,
wet with sweat and more odorous
than the forest's heart,
spurred them on
to the last gasp of the ascent,

promising that the summit would be
the only spring
to slake their parched throats.

»᾽Ω ᾽Ορθία·
ἔτοιμ᾽ ἡ φούχτα Σου
νὰ μάσει τὸ αἷμα τῶν πληγῶν,
καθὼς τοῦ ἀργάτη
ὁπού μαζώνει τὸ ρετσίνι
ἀπὸ τὸν κέδρον ἢ τὸν πεῦκο
πὄχει ἐπίτηδες σκιστεῖ!

»᾽Ω ᾽Ορθία·
ὅταν γαλήνια μόνη Σου ὁδηγᾶς,
σὰν ἡ γυναίκα τοῦ χωριάτη
μέσ᾽ ἀπὸ τοὺς κάμπους,
τὸ σκληρότερο πουλάρι νὰ βατέψει τὴ φοράδα
τὸ θεμελιακὸ δαμάλι τὴ γελάδα
καὶ στὴν ὀρθοτράχηλη τοῦ νόμου Σου παρθένα
ἐναντιωμένο κι ὅμοια ὑπάκοο
μὲ τὸ μέτωπο σκυφτὸ σὰν ἄτι
τὸν ἀνέγγιχτο πενταθλητή!

»Λιγόχορδο ἔταξες τὸ νόμο Σου·
τὸ Δώριον ἦχο ἄπαρτο τεῖχος!

»᾽Ω ᾽Ορθία·
τὰ λύγισ᾽ ὅλα ἡ ἐντολή Σου
ποὺ ἐπροβόδαε σὰ λιοντάρι στὸ πλευρὸ τοῦ ἀνθρώπου,
μὰ ἀπὸ πίσω του ἀκουλούθα ὡς κρυφοδάγκωτο σκυλὶ
σὰν οἱ παρθένες
μέθυες ἀπ᾽ τὴν πάλη,

O Orthia,
like the workman
who collects resin
from cedar or pine
incised for the purpose,
You hold Your cupped hand ready
to collect the blood from the wounds.

O Orthia,
as in the fields the peasant's wife leads
the fiercest colt to mount the mare,
the most splendid young bull to the cow,
so by Yourself You calmly lead
the virginal athlete,
resistant yet submissive,
his head bent like a stallion's,
to the proud virgin of Your rule.

The rule you gave has few chords:
the Doric mode is an unconquerable wall.

O Orthia,
Your command, leading man like a lion,
brought everything to heel
but, like the dog that bites in secret,
it also followed behind him
when the virgins,
drunk from the contest

81

στὰ λογγάρια τοῦ Ταϋγέτου
τ' ἀναμμένα δειλινά,
ὅμοια δαυλιὰ κρυμμένα στὴν ἀσβόλη,
μ' ἕνα ὑπάκοο βόγκο
σφιχτοκλειώντας τὴν ἀγκάλη
ἐσμίγανε ἀξεκόλλητα τὰ χείλια
γιὰ νὰ ξαλαφρώσουν τῆς παλαίστρας παρθενιᾶς τὸ βάρος
οἱ τριβάδες,

»ἐνῶ ἐδῶθε
στὸ καρτέρι
ὁ προεστὸς
ὁδήγαε στῆς γυναίκας του τὴν κλίνη
τὸ βαρὺ ἀθλητή,
στὴ γέρικη ἔγνοια του μονάχα ἕνα βλαστὸ τηρώντας
ὅμοιο μὲ τῶν Διόσκουρων τὸ δίδυμο ἄστρο
μὲ τὴν ἀλαφράδα τοῦ Ὑακίνθου
ἢ μὲ τοῦ Νηρέα τὴν ξωτικὴ ὀμορφιά!

»Ὢ Ὀρθία·
ὁπού ἔταξες λιμάνι τῆς καρδιᾶς Σου
τὴν ἀσύχαστη στὸ Ταίναρο τοῦ πόντου Σου ἁπλωσιὰ
ὁπού χοχλάζει
δέρνεται
βογγάει
»ὅσο κανένας Ὠκεανός,

82

in the forests of Taygetus
those hot evenings
like torches hidden in soot,
with a submissive groan
tightening their embrace,
locked lips to lips
so that their female partners might relieve them
of the weight of their virginity,

while here in Sparta,
the chief citizen
took in ambush the heavy athlete
and led him to his wife's bed,
his old mind visualizing only their offspring
like the twin star of the Dioscuri
with the lightness of Hyacinth
or the superb beauty of Nereus.*

O Orthia,
You who chose as Your heart's port
the restless expanse of Your sea at Taenarum,*
that seethes, struggles, moans
like no other Ocean,

» ὤ, πότε, πότε
μὲς στὰ σερπετὰ σκοτάδια τῶν κυμάτων
θὰ βουλιάξει καὶ θὰ πλέξει ἀγύριστα
τὸ θαμποκόκκινο αἷμα τῶν ὀχτρῶν;

» Ὤ, φύσα τέλος στὴν ψυχή μας τὴν ἀνατριχίλα Σου
πιὸ κρύα ἀπ' τοῦ χιονιᾶ
ποὺ ξαφνικὰ σαρώνει
ἀγεροπόταμος
ὅ, τι ἔβρει στὰ στενὰ φαράγγια Σου μπροστά!

» Ὤ, πότε τέλος,
Ὁδηγήτρα,
μὲ γυμνὸ ποδάρι δέρνοντας τὸ χιόνι ὁλονυχτίς,
θὰ ἰδοῦμε στὴν κορφή,
σὰν τὸ Βοριὰ
καὶ τὸ λιοντάρι
ποὺ τινάζεται ἀπ' τὸν ὕπνο,
τὴν ἀνατολή,

» σὰ μὲς στὸ φῶς
θὲ νὰ κριθεῖ ὁ ἀγώνας,
καὶ τ' ἀκρόνεα παλικάρια
θὰ κυλίσουν τὸν ἐνάντιο στὸ γκρεμό,
καὶ κάθε ζωὴ
θὰ θεριστεῖ στὸ χρυσὸ φῶς
» ὡς δίπλα ἀπ' τὸ χερόβολον ἡ παπαρούνα
ἀλόγιστα καὶ σιωπηλά;

when, when
will the enemies' dull red blood
sink and weave forever
into the crawling dark of the waves?

Inspire our soul at last with Your shudder
colder than the snow wind,
that river of air which suddenly sweeps
whatever it finds into Your narrow gorges.

O when, Huntress,
with naked foot beating the snow all night,
shall we see at last on the summit,
like Boreas
and the lion rousing himself from sleep,
the rising sun?

For in that light
the contest will be decided,
and the triumphant young men
will roll their opponents from the cliff top
and, like the poppy beside the sheaf,
each life
will be harvested in the golden light
spontaneously, silently.

» (Σύρε τὸν πόνο μέσαθέ μας
σὰν ὁ Ἡρακλῆς τὸν Κέρβερο ἀπ' τὸν Ἄδη,

» ὅταν ἁπλώνοντας στὸ χῶμα τὴν κοιλιά
καὶ μὲ σερνάμενα τὰ νύχια
ὁ Σκύλος ἀκολούθα, ἀξήγητα βαρύς,

» μὲ τὴν οὐρὰ στὰ σκέλια
καὶ τὸ μάτι ζαρωμένο ὀμπρὸς στὸν Ἥρωα
ὡς ἂν κοίταζε τὸν Ἥλιο!)

» Ὢ Ὀρθία!
Τοῦ μυστικοῦ Σου Ἀπόλλωνα τὴ γλήγορη κραυγὴ
τελείωνε
Σὺ ποὺ παραστέκεις
— ἡ ἀμάλαγη κ' ἡ ἀπάρθενη —
τὸ πάλεμα τῆς ἀγκαλιᾶς
καὶ τὴ στιγμὴ τῆς γέννας τὴν ἱερή!

» Δένε καὶ στέριωνε τὸ σπόρο
στὴν καρδιὰ τοῦ ἀντρός!

» Μὲς στὴν κοιλιὰ τῆς γυναικὸς
θεμέλιωνε τ' ἀρσενικά!»

86

(Draw out the pain from inside us
as Hercules drew Cerberus from Hades

when, settling his belly on the earth
and dragging his claws,
the Dog followed him, an inexplicable weight,

his tail beneath his haunches
and his eyes shrinking from the Hero
as though he gazed at the sun.)

O Orthia,
bring to an end
the sudden cry of Your mystic Apollo,
You who assist,
untouched and virginal,
in the struggle when bodies embrace
and at the sacred moment of birth.

Bind and rivet the seed
in the heart of man.

In the belly of woman
root the male."

ΔΑΙΔΑΛΟΣ

Μοίρα στὸν Ἴκαρο ἦταν νὰ πετάξει
καὶ νὰ χαθεῖ. . . Τὶ, ὡς ἦβρε σταφνισμένες
τὶς φοβερὲς τῆς λευτεριᾶς φτερούγες
ἀπ᾽ τὸν τρανὸ πατέρα του μπροστά του,
ἡ νιότη ἔριξε μόνη τὸ κορμί του
στὸν κίντυνο, κι ἂν ἴσως δὲν μπορούσε
τὸ μυστικό, τὸ ἁγνὸ τους νά ᾽βρει ζύγι!

Καὶ συνταράζει ἀρίζωτους ἀνθρώπους
στὸν πόνο, συνταράζει τὶς γυναῖκες,
πάνω ἀπ᾽ τὸ μέγα πέλαγο νὰ βλέπουν
ἐφηβικὸ κορμὶ σὰν ἕνας γλάρος
ν᾽ ἀνεμοδέρνεται ὄρθιο καὶ, ξάφνου,
νὰ χάνεται ἀπ᾽ τὰ μάτια τους.
                    Καὶ τότε,
τὴ θάλασσα ὅλη, λές, σὰν ἕνα δάκρυ
τὴ συλλογιοῦνται ἀτέλειωτο, σὰ θρῆνο
πυκνὸ πολύ, πού, τ᾽ ὄνομα τοῦ ἐφήβου
ὡς λέει καὶ ξαναλέει, ἀπὸ τὸ ἴδιο
παίρνει ψυχὴ καὶ νόημα κι ἄξιον ἦχο . . .

Μ᾽ ἂν ἄντρας πού, ἀπ᾽ τὴν πρώτην ἐλικιά του,
εἶπε οὐρανὸς καὶ γῆ πὼς ἦταν ἕνα,
καὶ στιὰ τοῦ κόσμου ἡ ἴδια ἡ συλλογή του·
κ᾽ εἶπε ποὺ ἡ γῆ νὰ σμίξει μὲ τ᾽ ἀστέρια
μπορεῖ, ὡς βαθὺ χωράφι μὲ χωράφι,
στάχυα νὰ θρέψει κι ὁ οὐρανός·

DAEDALUS*

The fate of Icarus could have been no other
than to fly and to perish. . . Because when he put on
freedom's awe-inspiring wings, their equipoise the art
of his great father, it was youth alone
that flung his body into danger, even if
he also failed, perhaps, to find their secret balance.

And men untried by suffering were shaken,
women were shaken, when over the huge sea
they saw an adolescent body upright
thresh the winds like a gull, and suddenly
plunge from sight.
            And then it was as if
they saw the whole sea like an endless teardrop,
a deep lament which, telling and retelling
the young boy's name, took from that name
soul and meaning and its own true sound.

But if a man who from his earliest years
has said that the heavens and the earth are one,
that his own thought is the world's hearth and center,
and that the earth may mingle with the stars
as a field's subsoil with its topsoil, so that the heavens too
may bring forth wheat;

ἂν ἄντρας
ποὺ εἶδε πῶς ὅλα σὲ ταφῆς εἰκόνα
τ' ἀνθρώπινα εἶναι, κ' οἱ ψυχὲς καὶ τὰ ἔργα·
κι ὅπως στ' ἀγάλματα ἔλυσε καὶ χέρια
καὶ πόδια, νὰ βαδίζουν μοναχά τους
στοὺς δρόμους τοῦ φωτός, ἀναλογίστη
καὶ τὶς καρδιὲς νὰ λύσει τῶν ἀνθρώπων·
κι ὡς, μὲ τρανὰ κορμιὰ δεντρῶν, καράβι
ἐστέριωσε θεϊκό, τὸ φόρτωσε ὅλο
ὄχι μ' ἐλέφαντα, ἤλεχτρο, ἢ χρυσάφι,
μά, ξεδιαλέοντας ἕνα κ' ἕνα, μ' ὅλους
τοὺς Ἥρωες, γιὰ τ' ἀθάνατα ταξίδια
τὰ μυθικά·
ἂν ἄντρας ποὺ κλεισμένος
στὴ φυλακὴ πόχτισε ὁ ἴδιος — ὅπως
ἡ κάμπια ὑφαίνει μόνη της τὸν τάφο
'ποὺ θὰ κλειστεῖ, ἀπ' τὸ θάνατο ζητώντας
ν' ἀλλάξει φύση σύρριζα — νειρεύτη,
στὰ βάθη τοῦ Λαβύρινθου, φτερούγες
πῶς φύτρωναν στοὺς ὤμους του, κι ἀγάλι
ἀγάλι ἡ πλήθια ἀγρύπνια του μετρήθη
μὲ τ' ὄνειρο, καὶ βγῆκε αὐτὴ νικήτρα·

σὰν εἶδε πάλι, ξάφνου, ὁλόγυρά του
ὄχλος θαμπὸς τὴ φοβερή του Τέχνη,
πού 'χε σημάδι της τὸ Θεό, νὰ θέλει
μιᾶς γνώμης ἀκαμάτρας τὸ στολίδι
νὰ γίνει·

                              if a man who has seen
that all human beings, their souls and their works,
lie in the grave's shadow, and has resolved
to set them free as already he has set free
the arms and legs of statues, so that they might walk
with their own motion along the paths of light;
who, just as he has ribbed the celestial ship
with the strong trunks of trees, has loaded it
not with ivory or amber or with gold
but with all the Heroes, chosen one by one
for the deathless voyages of myth;
                                        if a man
shut up in a prison built with his own hands—
as the caterpillar on its own will weave the tomb
in which it shuts itself, seeking through death
wholly to change its nature—if such a man
deep in the Labyrinth has dreamed that wings
have sprouted on his shoulders, and step by step
his waking mind has wrestled with the dream
until he has mastered it;

ἂν καὶ βαρὺ καὶ δουλεμένο
κορμὶ ἀπὸ μόχτο ἀπέραντον, ἐζώστη
τὶς φτερούγες σὰν ἄρματα, καὶ ὑψώθη
ἀργά — καὶ ἀνηφοροῦσε τοὺς ἀνέμους
θερίζοντάς τους ἥσυχα, ὅπως κόβει
μὲ τὸ δρεπάνι ὁ θεριστὴς μπροστά του
στὴ γῆ μεγάλα κύματα ἀπ᾽ ἀστάχυ —
πιὸ πάνω κι ἀπ᾽ τὸν ὄχλο, κι ἀπ᾽ τὸ κύμα
ποὺ τὸ παιδί του σκέπασε, πιὸ πάνω
κι ἀπ᾽ τοῦ πένθους τὰ σύνορα, νὰ σώσει
μὲ τὴν ψυχή του τὴν ψυχὴ τοῦ κόσμου·

μπορεῖ κι ἀρίζωτοι ἄνθρωποι στὸν πόνο,
μπορεῖ πικρὲς κι ἀδύναμες γυναῖκες,
ποὺ στὰ νεκροστολίσματα μονάχα
ἢ ἀπάνω στὰ νεκρόδειπνα μεράζουν
τὰ λόγια τους, νὰ ποῦν:
                        «Σκληρὸς πατέρας·
κι ἂν πρὸς τὴ δύση ἀρχίναγε νὰ γέρνει,
τὸ φοβερὸ ξακλούθησε ταξίδι,
τὴν ἔρμη ζωή του θέλοντας νὰ σώσει.»

Κι ἄλλοι μπορεῖ νὰ ποῦν:
                        «Τὸν κόσμο ἀφήνει
καὶ τὶς στρωτὲς συνήθειες τῶν ἀνθρώπων,
πράματ᾽ ἀδύνατα ζητώντας.»
                                Τέτοια

                              and though his body
is spent from all that strain, when he has seen
the dull crowd around him suddenly try to treat
his awe-inspiring Art, whose end was fixed in God,
as the mere bauble of an idle mind,
has girded those wings like armor, and slowly
has raised himself, has climbed among the winds,
reaping them peacefully as with his scythe
the reaper cuts in front of him great swaths of wheat
over the earth—has climbed above the crowd,
above the waves that swallowed up his child,
above even the frontiers of lament, to save
with his own soul the soul of the world:

                                        then
men untried by suffering, then women,
feeble and embittered women, who speak only
when laying out the dead or at the death-feast,
may both cry out:
                  "Harsh father, though his sun
was near its setting, still he kept his fearful course,
hoping to save his own pathetic life."

And others may exclaim:
                        "He leaves the world,
leaves the settled ways of men, and goes
in search of the impossible."

νὰ ποῦν μπορεῖ . . .
                Μὰ ἐσὺ, τρανὲ πατέρα,
πατέρα ὅλων ἐμᾶς ὁποὺ σὲ εἰκόνα
ταφῆς, ἀπὸ τὴν πρώτην ἐλικιά μας,
ἔχουμε ἰδεῖ τὰ πάντα καί, ἢ μὲ λόγο
ἢ μὲ σμιλάρι, μὲ τὴν πνοή μας ὅλη
ἀπάνω ἀπ' τὸ ρυθμὸ τὸ σαρκοφάγο
νὰ ὑψωθοῦμε ἀγωνιόμαστε·
                        ὦ πατέρα,
ποὺ καὶ γιὰ μᾶς γῆ κι οὐρανὸς εἶν' ἕνα,
καὶ στιὰ τοῦ κόσμου ἡ ἴδια ἡ συλλογή μας,
καὶ λέμε ἡ γῆ νὰ σμίξει μὲ τ' ἀστέρια
μπορεῖ, ὡς βαθὺ χωράφι μὲ χωράφι,
στάχυα νὰ θρέψει κι ὁ οὐρανός·
                        πατέρα,
τὶς ὦρες ποὺ βαραίνει στὴν καρδιά μας
τῆς ζωῆς ἡ πίκρα μ' ὅλο της τὸ βάρος,
καὶ δὲ σηκώνει ἡ νιότη τὴν ὁρμή μας,
μὰ ἡ Θέληση ποὺ ἀπάνω κι ἀπ' τοὺς τάφους
ὀρθὴ ἀγρυπνᾶ, τὶ στὸ δικό της μάτι
καὶ ἡ θάλασσα ρηχή, ποὺ τοὺς πνιγμένους
σφιχτοκρατάει καὶ δὲν τοὺς δίνει πίσω,
ρηχὴ καὶ ἡ γῆ ὅπου οἱ νεκροὶ κοιμοῦνται·

τὶς ὦρες τοῦ ὄρθρου, ποὺ μοχτοῦμε ἀκόμα,
σὰν κ' οἱ νεκροὶ κ' οἱ ζωντανοὶ πλαγιάζουν
στὸν ἴδιο ἀνόνειρο ἢ βαριόνειρο ὕπνο,
μὴ σταματᾶς νὰ ὑψώνεσαι μπροστά μας
σκαλώνοντας μὲ ἀργές, στρωτὲς φτερούγες
τὸν οὐρανὸ τῆς Σκέψης μας ὁλοένα,
Δαίδαλε αἰώνιε, ἀπόκοσμος Ἑωσφόρος!

So they may talk.
But you, great father, father of all of us
who from our earliest years have seen that everything
lies in the grave's shadow and who, with words
or chisel, have struggled with all our spirit
to rise above this flesh-consuming rhythm:
                                        father,
since for us too the earth and the heavens are one
and our own thought is the world's hearth and center,
since we also say that earth may mingle with the stars
as a field's subsoil with its topsoil, so that the heavens too
may bring forth wheat:
                        father, at those times
when life's bitterness weighs with its full burden
on our hearts, and our strength can be roused no more by youth
but only by the Will that stands watchful
even over the grave, because to It the sea
which hugs the drowned remorselessly is itself shallow,
and shallow too the earth where the dead sleep;

in the dawn hours, as still we struggle on,
while the living and the dead both lie in the same
dreamless or dream-laden slumber, do not stop
ascending in front of us, but climb always
with slow even wings the heavens of our Thought,
eternal Daedalus, Dawnstar of the Beyond.

Η ΑΥΤΟΚΤΟΝΙΑ ΤΟΥ ΑΤΖΕΣΙΒΑΝΟ
ΜΑΘΗΤΗ ΤΟΥ ΒΟΥΔΑ

᾽Ανεπίληπτα ἐπῆρε τὸ μαχαίρι
ὁ ᾽Ατζεσιβάνο. Κ᾽ ἤτανε ἡ ψυχή του
τὴν ὥρα ἐκείνη ὁλάσπρο περιστέρι.
Κι ὅπως κυλᾶ, ἀπὸ τ᾽ ἄδυτα τοῦ ἀδύτου
τῶν οὐρανῶν, μὲς στὴ νυχτιὰ ἕν᾽ ἀστέρι,
ἤ, ὡς πέφτει ἀνθὸς μηλιᾶς μὲ πράο ἀγέρι,
ἔτσι ἀπ᾽ τὰ στήθη πέταξε ἡ πνοή του.

Χαμένοι τέτοιοι θάνατοι δὲν πᾶνε.
Γιατὶ μονάχα ἐκεῖνοι π᾽ ἀγαπᾶνε
τὴ ζωὴ στὴ μυστική της πρώτη ἀξία,
μποροῦν καὶ νὰ θερίσουνε μονάχοι
τῆς ὕπαρξής τους τὸ μεγάλο ἀστάχυ,
ποὺ γέρνει πιά, μὲ θείαν ἀταραξία!

96

THE SUICIDE OF ATZESIVANO
DISCIPLE OF BUDDHA

Irreproachably Atzesivano
took up the knife, his soul
at that moment a white pigeon.
And as a star at night
glides from the sky's inmost sanctuary
or as an apple blossom falls in the gentle breeze,
so his spirit took wing from his breast.

Deaths like this are not wasted.
Because only those who love life
in its mystical first glory
can reap by themselves
the great harvest of their existence—
spent now—with a divine tranquillity.

ΙΕΡΑ ΟΔΟΣ

Ἀπὸ τὴ νέα πληγὴ ποὺ μ' ἄνοιξεν ἡ μοίρα
ἔμπαιν' ὁ ἥλιος, θαρρῶσα, στὴν καρδιά μου
μὲ τόση ὁρμή, καθὼς βασίλευε, ὅπως
ἀπὸ ραγισματιὰν αἰφνίδια μπαίνει
τὸ κύμα σὲ καράβι π' ὁλοένα
βουλιάζει. Γιατὶ ἐκεῖνο πιὰ τὸ δείλι,
σὰν ἄρρωστος, καιρό, ποὺ πρωτοβγαίνει
ν' ἀρμέξει ζωὴ ἀπ' τὸν ἔξω κόσμον, ἤμουν
περπατητὴς μοναχικὸς στὸ δρόμο
ποὺ ξεκινᾶ ἀπὸ τὴν Ἀθήνα κ' ἔχει
σημάδι του ἱερὸ τὴν Ἐλευσίνα.
Τὶ ἦταν γιὰ μένα αὐτὸς ὁ δρόμος πάντα
σὰ δρόμος τῆς Ψυχῆς. Φανερωμένος
μεγάλος ποταμός, κυλοῦσε ἐδῶθε
ἀργὰ συρμένα ἀπὸ τὰ βόδια ἁμάξια
γεμάτα ἀθεμωνιὲς ἢ ξύλα, κι ἄλλα
ἁμάξια, γοργὰ ποὺ προσπερνοῦσαν,
μὲ τοὺς ἀνθρώπους μέσα τους σὰν ἴσκιους.

Μὰ παραπέρα, σὰ νὰ χάθη ὁ κόσμος
κ' ἔμειν' ἡ φύση μόνη, ὥρα κι ὥρα
μιὰν ἡσυχία βασίλεψε. Κ' ἡ πέτρα
π' ἀντίκρισα σὲ μιὰ ἄκρη ριζωμένη,
θρονὶ μοῦ φάνη μοιραμένο μου ἦταν
ἀπ' τοὺς αἰῶνες. Κ' ἔπλεξα τὰ χέρια,
σὰν κάθισα, στὰ γόνατα, ξεχνώντας
ἂν κίνησα τὴ μέρα αὐτὴ ἢ ἂν πῆρα
αἰῶνες πίσω αὐτὸ τὸν ἴδιο δρόμο.

98

THE SACRED WAY*

Through the new wound that fate had opened in me
I felt the setting sun flood my heart
with a force like that of water when it pours
through a hole in a sinking ship.
                                    Because again,
like one long sick when he first ventures forth
to milk life from the outside world, I walked
alone at dusk along the road that starts
at Athens and for its destination has
the sanctuary at Eleusis—the road
that for me was always the Soul's road. It bore,
like a huge river, carts slowly drawn by oxen,
loaded with sheaves or wood, and other carts
that quickly passed me by, the people in them
shadowlike.

            But farther on, as if the world
had disappeared and nature alone was left,
unbroken stillness reigned. And the rock I found
rooted at the roadside seemed like a throne
long predestined for me. And as I sat
I folded my hands over my knees, forgetting if
it was today that I'd set out or if
I'd taken this same road centuries before.

Μὰ νά· στὴν ἡσυχία αὐτή, ἀπ' τὸ γύρο
τὸν κοντινό, προβάλανε τρεῖς ἴσκιοι.
Ἕνας Ἀτσίγγανος ἀγνάντια ἐρχόνταν,
καὶ πίσωθέ του ἀκλούθααν, μ' ἀλυσίδες
συρμένες, δυὸ ἀργοβάδιστες ἀρκοῦδες.

Καὶ νά· ὡς σὲ λίγο ζύγωσαν μπροστά μου
καὶ μ' εἶδε ὁ Γύφτος, πρὶν καλὰ προφτάσω
νὰ τὸν κοιτάξω, τράβηξε ἀπ' τὸν ὦμο
τὸ ντέφι καί, χτυπώντας το μὲ τό 'να
χέρι, μὲ τ' ἄλλον ἔσυρε μὲ βία
τὶς ἀλυσίδες. Κ' οἱ δυὸ ἀρκοῦδες τότε
στὰ δυὸ τους σκώθηκαν, βαριά.
                                    Ἡ μία,
(ἤτανε ἡ μάνα, φανερά), ἡ μεγάλη,
μὲ πλεχτὲς χάντρες ὅλο στολισμένο
τὸ μέτωπο γαλάζιες, κι ἀπὸ πάνω
μιὰν ἄσπρη ἀβασκαντήρα, ἀνασηκώθη
ξάφνου τρανή, σὰν προαιώνιο νά 'ταν
ξόανο Μεγάλης Θεᾶς, τῆς αἰώνιας Μάνας,
αὐτῆς τῆς ἴδιας ποὺ ἱερὰ θλιμμένη,
μὲ τὸν καιρὸν ὡς πῆρε ἀνθρώπινη ὄψη,
γιὰ τὸν καημὸ τῆς κόρης της λεγόνταν
Δήμητρα ἐδῶ, γιὰ τὸν καημὸ τοῦ γιοῦ της
πιὸ πέρα ἦταν Ἀλκμήνη ἢ Παναγία.
Καὶ τὸ μικρὸ στὸ πλάγι της ἀρκούδι,
σὰ μεγάλο παιχνίδι, σὰν ἀνίδεο
μικρὸ παιδί, ἀνασκώθηκε κ' ἐκεῖνο
ὑπάκοο, μὴ μαντεύοντας ἀκόμα
τοῦ πόνου του τὸ μάκρος, καὶ τὴν πίκρα
τῆς σκλαβιᾶς, ποὺ καθρέφτιζεν ἡ μάνα
στὰ δυὸ πυρά της ποὺ τὸ κοίτααν μάτια!

But then, rounding the nearest bend, three shadows
entered this stillness: a gypsy and, after him,
dragged by their chains, two heavy-footed bears.

And then, as they drew near to me, the gypsy,
before I'd really noticed him, saw me,
took his tambourine down from his shoulder,
struck it with one hand, and with the other tugged
fiercely at the chains. And the two bears
rose on their hind legs heavily.
                                        One of them,
the larger—clearly she was the mother—
her head adorned with tassels of blue beads
crowned by a white amulet, towered up
suddenly enormous, as if she were
the primordial image of the Great Goddess,
the Eternal Mother, sacred in her affliction,
who, in human form, was called Demeter
here at Eleusis, where she mourned her daughter,
and elsewhere, where she mourned her son,
was called Alcmene or the Holy Virgin.
And the small bear at her side, like a big toy,
like an innocent child, also rose up, submissive,
not sensing yet the years of pain ahead
or the bitterness of slavery mirrored
in the burning eyes his mother turned on him.

101

'Αλλ' ὡς ἀπὸ τὸν κάματον ἐκείνη
ὀκνοῦσε νὰ χορέψει, ὁ Γύφτος, μ' ἔνα
πιδέξιο τράβηγμα τῆς ἀλυσίδας
στοῦ μικροῦ τὸ ρουθούνι, ματωμένο
ἀκόμα ἀπ' τὸ χαλκὰ ποὺ λίγες μέρες
φαινόνταν πὼς τοῦ τρύπησεν, αἰφνίδια
τὴν ἔκαμε, μουγκρίζοντας μὲ πόνο,
νὰ ὀρθώνεται ψηλά, πρὸς τὸ παιδί της
γυρνώντας τὸ κεφάλι, καὶ νὰ ὀρχιέται
ζωηρά.
            Κ' ἐγώ, ὡς ἐκοίταζα, τραβοῦσα
ἔξω ἀπ' τὸ χρόνο, μακριὰ ἀπ' τὸ χρόνο,
ἐλεύτερος ἀπὸ μορφὲς κλεισμένες
στὸν καιρό, ἀπὸ ἀγάλματα κ' εἰκόνες·
ἤμουν ἔξω, ἤμουν ἔξω ἀπὸ τὸ χρόνο.

Μὰ μπροστά μου, ὀρθωμένη ἀπὸ τὴ βία
τοῦ χαλκᾶ καὶ τῆς ἄμοιρης στοργῆς της,
δὲν ἔβλεπα ἄλλο ἀπ' τὴν τρανὴν ἀρκούδα
μὲ τὶς γαλάζιες χάντρες στὸ κεφάλι,
μαρτυρικὸ τεράστιο σύμβολο ὅλου
τοῦ κόσμου, τωρινοῦ καὶ περασμένου,
μαρτυρικὸ τεράστιο σύμβολο ὅλου
τοῦ πόνου τοῦ πανάρχαιου, ὁπ' ἀκόμα
δὲν τοῦ πληρώθη ἀπ' τοὺς θνητοὺς αἰῶνες
ὁ φόρος τῆς ψυχῆς.
                        Τὶ ἐτούτη ἀκόμα
ἦταν κ' εἶναι στὸν Ἅδη.
                                    Καὶ σκυμμένο
τὸ κεφάλι μου κράτησα ὁλοένα,
καθὼς στὸ ντέφι μέσα ἔριχνα, σκλάβος
κ' ἐγὼ τοῦ κόσμου, μιὰ δραχμή.

102

But because she, dead tired, was slow to dance,
the gypsy, with a single dexterous jerk
of the chain hanging from the young bear's nostril—
bloody still from the ring that had pierced it
perhaps a few days before—made the mother,
groaning with pain, abruptly straighten up
and then, her head turning toward her child,
dance vigorously.
                    And I, as I watched, was drawn
outside and far from time, free from forms
closed within time, from statues and images.
I was outside, I was beyond time.

And in front of me I saw nothing except
the large bear, with the blue beads on her head,
raised by the ring's wrench and her ill-fated tenderness,
huge testifying symbol
of all the world, the present and the past,
huge testifying symbol
of all primaeval suffering for which,
throughout the human centuries, the soul's
tax has still not been paid. Because the soul
has been and still is in Hell.
                        And I,
who am also slave to this world,
kept my head lowered as I threw a coin
into the tambourine.

Μὰ ὡς, τέλος,
ὁ Ἀτσίγγανος ξεμάκρυνε, τραβῶντας
ξανὰ τὶς δυὸ ἀργοβάδιστες ἀρκοῦδες,
καὶ χάθηκε στὸ μούχρωμα, ἡ καρδιά μου
μὲ σήκωσε νὰ ξαναπάρω πάλι
τὸ δρόμον ὁποὺ τέλειωνε στὰ ρείπια
τοῦ Ἱεροῦ τῆς Ψυχῆς, στὴν Ἐλευσίνα.
Κ᾿ ἡ καρδιά μου, ὡς ἐβάδιζα, βογκοῦσε:
«Θά ᾿ρτει τάχα ποτέ, θὲ νά ᾿ρτει ἡ ὥρα
ποὺ ἡ ψυχὴ τῆς ἀρκούδας καὶ τοῦ Γύφτου,
κ᾿ ἡ ψυχή μου, ποὺ Μνημένη τηνε κράζω,
θὰ γιορτάσουν μαζί;»
                          Κι ὡς προχωροῦσα,
καὶ βράδιαζε, ξανάνιωσα ἀπ᾿ τὴν ἴδια
πληγή, ποὺ ἡ μοίρα μ᾿ ἄνοιξε, τὸ σκότος
νὰ μπαίνει ὁρμητικὰ μὲς στὴν καρδιά μου,
καθὼς ἀπὸ ραγισματιὰν αἰφνίδια μπαίνει
τὸ κύμα σὲ καράβι ποὺ ὁλοένα
βουλιάζει. Κι ὅμως τέτοια ὡς νὰ διψοῦσε
πλημμύραν ἡ καρδιά μου, σὰ βυθίστη
ὡς νὰ πνίγηκε ἀκέρια στὰ σκοτάδια,
σὰ βυθίστηκε ἀκέρια στὰ σκοτάδια,
ἕνα μούρμουρο ἁπλώθη ἀπάνωθέ μου,
ἕνα μούρμουρο,
                 κ᾿ ἔμοιαζ᾿ ἔλεε:
                                    «Θά ᾿ρτει.»

Then, as the gypsy
at last went on his way, again dragging
the slow-footed bears behind him, and vanished
in the dusk, my heart prompted me once more
to take the road that terminates among
the ruins of the Soul's temple, at Eleusis.
And as I walked my heart asked in anguish:
"Will the time, the moment ever come when the bear's soul
and the gypsy's and my own, that I call initiated,
will feast together?"
                            And as I moved on, night fell,
and again through the wound that fate had opened in me
I felt the darkness flood my heart as water
pours through a hole in a sinking ship.
Yet when—as though it had been thirsting for that flood—
my heart sank down completely into the darkness,
sank completely as though to drown in the darkness,
a murmur spread through all the air above me,
a murmur,
                and it seemed to say:
                                    "It will come."

ΑΤΤΙΚΟ

Στὰ δυό μας τ' ἄλογα, ἀδερφέ,
τὸ μαυροχήτη 'Αρίωνα
καὶ τὸν ξανθὸ Δημογοργόνα, πὰ στὴ στάλα
τοῦ ἀθάνατου μεσημεριοῦ,
στῆς 'Ελευσίνας τριποδίζαμε τὸ δρόμο,
κουβεντιάζοντας ἀργά,
σὰ δυὸ παλιοὶ ἱερεῖς τῶν 'Αθηναίων, καβάλα . . .

«Μὴν εἶναι τάχα χίμαιρα;
Δὲ βλέπω ἀπὸ τὸ φῶς τὸ μετρημένο
μὰ ἀπὸ τὴν ἄσωτη ἀστραπὴ
ποὺ μ' ἔχει ἀπὸ παντοῦθε τυλιγμένο . . .

» 'Ο χρόνος ποῦ εἶναι; 'Απὸ τὰ φρένα μου
μιὰν αὔρα λιγοστὴ τὸν ἔχει πάρει . . .
Τὰ πεῦκα τοῦτα εἶν' ἀπὸ πάντα, κ' ἡ πνοὴ
αἰώνια ἀπ' τὸ νιό, ποὺ πνέει, θυμάρι . . .

» Κ' ἐτοῦτος ὁ ρυθμός, ποὺ τριποδίζουμε,
σὰ νά 'ναι ὁ ἴδιος ὁ ρυθμὸς π' ἀκόμα
τ' ἄτια τὰ ἀρχαῖα ἀφήκανε τὸ χνάρι του
θαμπὸ πάνω στὸ θεῖον ἐτοῦτο χῶμα . . .»

«Τὸ σῶμα μόνο, ποὺ ἀπ' τὸ θάνατο νὰ βγεῖ
μπορεῖ, βολεῖ νὰ ἰδεῖ καὶ ν' ἀντικρίσει
τὴ γῆν αὐτὴ μέσα σὲ τούτη τὴ σιγή·
τὸ νικητήριο σῶμα, ποὺ θὰ λύσει

ATTIC

Astride our two horses, brother,
black-maned Arion
and bay Demogorgon, at the precipitation*
of immortal noon,
we ambled along the road to Eleusis*
talking slowly
like two ancient priests of Athens on horseback. . .

"Can this be an illusion?
I don't see by measured light
but by an unlimited brilliance
that has wrapped me around on all sides.

Where is time? The lightest breeze
has taken time out of my mind.
These pines are forever, the breath
wafted by the young thyme eternal.

And the rhythm of our horses now
seems the same rhythm that still lives
under obscure hoofprints of ancient horses
left in this same holy ground."

"Only that body which can escape from death
will see and encounter
this earth in this silence:
the triumphant body which can loosen

107

» καὶ τὰ στερνὰ ποὺ τὸ τυλίγανε δεσμά,
καθὼς τὸ γνέμα τους οἱ κάμπιες, κι ὡς τὴ σκέψη
τ᾽ ἀνθρώπου ὁ νοῦς, ὥσπου σ᾽ ἐκεῖνες τὰ φτερά
ν᾽ ἀνθίσουν, καὶ στὸν ἄνθρωπον ἡ μέσα βλέψη . . .

» Ὄχι, δὲν εἶναι χίμαιρα
νὰ καβαλᾶμε τ᾽ ὄνειρο τὴ θείαν ἐτούτη μέρα
ποὺ ὅλα, ὁρατὰ κι ἀόρατα, κ᾽ ἐμεῖς καὶ τ᾽ ἄτια μας κ᾽ οἱ θεοί,
στὴν ἴδια πνέμε μέσα κρουσταλλένια σφαίρα!»

«Ἂς μὴν ξυπνοῦσα ἀπ᾽ τ᾽ ὄνειρον αὐτό . . .
Σὰ φτάσουμε στὴ θάλασσα, τὴν ὥρα
ποὺ ἀπὸ τὴ ζέστα, τ᾽ ἄλογά μας σπιρουνίζοντας,
θὰ σπρώξουμε τὰ στήθια τους σὰν πλώρα

» στὸ κύμα μέσα, νὰ ξυπνήσουμε μπορεῖ
στοῦ χρόνου τ᾽ ἀντισκόμματα καὶ πάλι,
καὶ νὰ σκορπίσουμε τὸ θάμα ἀνάμεσα
στὴ μυστικὴ ἀναγάλλια καὶ στὴν πλήθια πάλη . . .»

«Ἀκόμα ζεῖς τὴ μερασμένη ὁρμή,
ἀδερφέ; Καὶ μέσ᾽ ἀπ᾽ τὸ φτενὸ τό χῶμα
τῆς γῆς αὐτῆς, ἀκόμα δὲν ἐλύτρωσες
τὸ μυστικὰ κατορθωμένο σῶμα,

» σὰν τὸ τζιτζίκι ποὺ ἀπ᾽ τὸν τάφο βγαίνοντας,
στὸ πιὸ ἀψηλὸ θρονιάζοντας κλωνάρι,
τὴ γῆ βιγλίζει καὶ τὸν ἥλιο καὶ τοὺς θεοὺς
μ᾽ ἕνα λιτὸ ἀναστάσιμο τροπάρι;

even the last bonds that coiled around it,
as a chrysalis its cocoon and man's mind
his thought, until for the chrysalis wings blossom
and for man the inner vision dawns.

No, it's not an illusion
for us to ride a dream on this godlike day
when everything, visible and invisible, we and our horses
        and the gods too,
breathe inside the same crystal sphere!"

"May I never wake from this dream . . .
When we reach the sea—the heat
moving us to spur our horses
and to press them forward, prowlike,

into the waves—we may then wake up
again within time's contradictions
and split the miracle between
hidden exultation and the multifarious struggle."

"Do you still live with a divided impulse,
brother? Haven't you yet freed
from the fine soil of this earth
the body that is mystically consummated,

like the cicada rising from the tomb
to settle on the highest branch,
watching over the earth, the sun and the gods,
with a simple hymn of resurrection?

109

» Μὰ ἐμεῖς, ὁποὺ τὸ θάνατο νικήσαμε, ἀδερφέ,
τόσες φορές, καὶ ποὺ διαλύσαμε τὰ σκότη
τέτοιων καιρῶν, τραβᾶμε τώρα γιὰ τὸ ἀμέριστο,
κι ὁλοένα, λέω, γινόμαστε πιὸ νιοὶ κι ἀπὸ τὴ νιότη !

» Κι αὐτὸ ποὺ δὲν τὸ βλέπουμεν ἐμεῖς
ἀκόμα, ἴσως καὶ τ᾽ ἄτια μας νὰ τὸ μαντεύουν
μπορεῖ, πού, νά, ἀρχινᾶν μεσοδρομὶς
τὸ χαλινάρι νὰ μασᾶν καὶ νὰ χορεύουν

» ἀνάλαφρα, σὰ νὰ γυρεύουν ξαφνικὰ
ν᾽ ἀλλάξουνε τὸ πάτημα καί, στὴν παλιὰν ἐτούτη ρούγα,
— τὸ χαλινάρι κράταγε, ἀδερφέ, κι ὀμπρός ! —,
τὸν καλπασμό τους νὰ τὸν κάμουνε φτερούγα.

» Ὄχι, δὲν εἶναι χίμαιρα
νὰ καβαλᾶμε τ᾽ ὄνειρο τὴ θείαν ἐτούτη μέρα,
ποὺ ὅλα, ὁρατὰ κι ἀόρατα, κ᾽ ἐμεῖς, καὶ οἱ ἥρωες, κ᾽ οἱ θεοί,
στὴν ἴδια ὁρμᾶμε μέσα αἰώνια σφαίρα ! »

110

But we who have so often triumphed over death,
brother, and have dispelled the darkness
of times like these, now travel toward the indivisible
and become, continually, younger than youth itself!

And that which we still don't see
perhaps our horses can divine
because, look, in mid-stride they've begun
to chew their bits, prance, tread

the air, as though all of a sudden they want
to change their gait and, in this ancient lane
—grip your bridle, brother, and let them go!—
transform their gallop into winged flight.

No, it's not an illusion
for us to ride a dream on this godlike day
when everything, visible and invisible, we and the heroes
    and the gods too,
move forward inside the same eternal sphere!"

111

IV

Κράτα τὸ χέρι μου· σὲ λίγο θὰ διαβοῦμε
τὸν κάβο, ποὺ ἡ βοή του ἀχολογάει μακράθε
σὰν ἔνας κόσμος πα' στὰ βράχια του νὰ καταλνέται!
Μὰ Ἐσύ, τὸ χέρι κράτα μου σφιχτά, ὥς νὰ νιώσεις
τῆς καρδιᾶς μου τὸ χτύπο ν' ἀνεβαίνει
μέσ' ἀπ' τὶς φλέβες Σου ὥσμε τῆς ψυχῆς Σου
τὰ βάθη, καὶ τὸ πέλαο νὰ δαμάζει
ὁποὺ ἡ ἀχτή του εἶν' ἄσπρα κόκαλα γιομάτη!
Κράτα σφιχτὰ τὸ χέρι μου καὶ νιῶσε
τὸ θεοτικὸ προαίσθημα νὰ ὑψώνει
τὸ μυστικό του κύμα ἀπάνω ἀπ' ὅλα,
καὶ μὴ μὲ λόγια ἢ μ' ἔννοια τὸ μποδίζεις,
ἀλλὰ τὸ νοῦ Σου ἀκούμπαγε στὸ νοῦ μου,
σὰ σύννεφα πού, τό 'να πλάι ἀπ' τ' ἄλλο
ὡς ἀκουμπᾶνε, μιὰ ἀστραπὴ τὰ σμίγει
μὲς σ' ἔνα φῶς θαμπωτικό, κι ἀμέσως
ἔτσι σμιχτὰ τὰ ὑψώνει ὡς τὴν πηγή τους!...

Κράτα τὸ χέρι μου σφιχτά, ἂν ἀλήθεια
ἐκεῖθε λαχταρᾶς νὰ προσδιαβοῦμε
ἀπ' τὰ πικρὰ τὰ μέτρα τῶν ἀνθρώπων,
στοῦ Ρυθμοῦ τὴν κορφήν, ὁπού 'ναι ἡ ἴδια
τοῦ κίνδυνου ἡ κορφή, τὸ διαβασίδι
τοῦ ἴδιου τοῦ Θανάτου, ἀπ' ὅπου ἀρχίζει
—ὦ θεοτικὸ προμήνυμα—ἡ μεγάλη
τῆς λευτεριᾶς ἡ θάλασσα, ποὺ μόνη
κυλάει τρανά, πλατιά, τὰ σμάραγδά της
πρὸς τὸν ὕστατο πόλο!
                                    Ὦ, μὴν ἀφήνεις
τὸ χέρι μου, Σ' τὸ δέομαι, μὴν τ' ἀφήνεις!

112

LETTER IV

Hold my hand; soon we'll be rounding the cape
thundering in the distance as though a whole
world is coming apart against its rocks.
Hold my hand tightly until You feel my heartbeat
rising through Your veins into Your soul's depths,
taming the sea, its shores spread with white bones.
Hold my hand tightly and feel the godlike
premonition raising its secret wave
above all else, and do not hinder it
with words or thought, but lay Your mind on my mind
like clouds that lie the one against the other
until a flash of lightning fuses them
in a blinding dazzle and, mingled like this,
raises them instantly to their source.

Hold my hand firmly if You really long
to mount with me beyond man's bitter limits
and reach Rhythm's highest peak, the peak
of danger too, the pass of Death itself,
the source—O godly omen—from which the great
sea of freedom spreads, huge, powerful,
rolling its emeralds with its own surge toward
the ultimate pole. O don't, don't let go
of my hand, I beg You, don't let go of it.

113

ΜΕΛΕΤΗ ΘΑΝΑΤΟΥ

Τέλος κι ἀρχὴν ἡ μνήμη ἐδῶ δὲν ἔχει . . .

Στεφάνι ἄλικα ρόδα ἦταν ἡ θέρμη
στὸ μέτωπό μου ὁλόγυρα, στεφάνι
σφιχτό, ποὺ νὰ τὸ βγάλω δὲν μπορούσα,
καὶ παραμίλημα ἱερὸ βαθιά μου,
τὴν ὥρα π' ἀπ' τὴν ἄγια πύλη τοῦ ἴσκιου,
μὲς στὴν ἀχλὺν ὁπού 'χα βυθισμένα
τὰ βλέφαρα, μισάνοιξες τὴ θύρα,
μὲ τὰ μαλλιὰ λυτά, ὄχι ὅπως φτάνει
θρηνητική, πικρὴ μοιρολογήτρα,
ἀπάνω ἀπὸ τὸ σῶμα μου νὰ κλάψεις
ποὺ στὴν καινούργιαν ἄνοιξη ἁπλωνόνταν
σάμπως νεκρὸ στὴν κλίνη μου·
                            ἀλλὰ ὅπως,
μέρες πολλὲς πρωτύτερα, ἡ Ἀστάρτη
τὸ κορμί της ἐτοίμαζε γιὰ νά μπει
μέσα στὸν Ἅδη ὁλάκερη, νὰ μπάσει
τοῦ κορμιοῦ της τὸ φῶς μέσα στὸν Ἅδη,
νὰ λάμψει ἀπ' τὸ κορμί της ὅλος ὁ Ἅδης·

καὶ μετροῦσε γαλήνια τὶς ἡμέρες
τῆς τρανῆς της θεϊκιᾶς δοκιμασίας,
τρεῖς μέρες γιὰ τὴ νήστεια, κι ἄλλες τόσες
γιὰ νὰ πλυθεῖ στὶς θεῖες πηγὲς ἀκέρια,
γιὰ νὰ λουστεῖ, νὰ εὐφράνει τὴν κορφή της,
νὰ χτενιστεῖ, τὰ χείλη της νὰ βάψει,
κι ἀφοῦ ντυθεῖ μ' ἑφτὰ στολές, ὁποὺ ὅμοιες
μὲ πλανῆτες ἡ μιὰ πάνω ἀπ' τὴν ἄλλη
γύρ' ἀπ' τὴ θεία της γύμνια ἀργοδινοῦνταν,
νὰ κατεβεῖ σκαλὶ σκαλὶ τὰ Ἐρέβη,

REHEARSING FOR DEATH*

Memory has no end here and no beginning . . .

The fever was a crown of scarlet roses
around my forehead, a crown so tightly fixed
I could not take it off, and a holy
delirium had risen up inside me,
when You, in the shadow's sacred gateway,
in the haze where my eyelids were immersed,
half-opened the door, Your hair loose, arriving
not as a bitter mourner, all lamentation,
to weep in early spring over my body
where it lay stretched out corpselike on my bed,
but as Astarte, who days ahead prepared
her body so that she might enter Hades with it,
might bring her body's light to Hades,
to make all Hades radiant with her body;

and serenely she reviewed the days
of her great, her godlike trial: three days
to fast, three more to wash herself completely
in the sacred springs, to wash her hair,
bring her head delight, to comb and brush it,
paint her lips; and when she'd dressed herself
in seven robes, the one over the other
slowly revolving like planets around
her divine nakedness, she would then go down
step by step into the Darkness, throwing off

μπροστὰ ἀπὸ κάθε πύλη παραιτώντας
κι ἀπὸ τὴ μιὰ στολήν, ὥσπου στὸ βάθος,
τὸ ὕστερο βάθος τὸ ἱερό, νὰ μπάσει
τὸ ἀνέσπερό της φῶς μέσα στὸν Ἅδη,
νὰ καταλύσει ἡ γύμνια της τὸν Ἅδη·

ὅμοια κ᾽ ἐσὺ κατέβης ὡς σ᾽ ἐμένα,
ἑτοιμασμένη, κι ἅπλωσες σιμά μου,
βουβὴ ξαπλώθης κι ἄσειστη σιμά μου,
καὶ καταλύθη ὁ Ἅδης στὴν καρδιά μου,
κ᾽ ἔγινε ἀνάσταση καὶ νίκη ὁ Ἅδης,
καὶ πῆρα τὸ τρανὸ μαργαριτάρι
στὴ φούχτα μου, καὶ πῆρα στὴν καρδιά μου
τὴν ἄνοιξη, καὶ τ᾽ ἄλικα τὰ ρόδα
τῆς θέρμης τά ᾽νιωσα ἄξαφνα ἕνα στέμμα,
κ᾽ ἡ μαύρη κλίνη μου ἔγινε καράβι,
τοῦ Θεοῦ καράβι ἀσπέδιστο, κι ὁ μόχτος
τοῦ νοῦ μου ἀρμενιστὴς στὴ μέση ἀπ᾽ τ᾽ ἄστρα.

Ἄ, δὲν ξαπλώθηκε ἔτσι ἡ Σουλαμίτις,
τοῦ Δαβὶδ νὰ ζεστάνει μὲς στὴν κλίνη
τὰ παγωμένα μέλη, τοῦ προφήτη
καὶ βασιλιᾶ Δαβὶδ ποὺ τοῦ ᾽χε ἀφήσει
τὸ πνέμα του ὁ ψαλμός, κι ἀπ᾽ τὴν καρδιά του
ἐξανεμίστη ἡ ἅγια ἀντρίκεια ζέστη
ποὺ βασιλιὰ τὸν ξύπναε καὶ προφήτη,
κι ἀγωνιστὴ καὶ χορευτή, καὶ πρῶτο
γύρα στοῦ Θεοῦ τὴν κιβωτὸ προμάχο·

116

a robe at each gate until, in the depths,
in the ultimate holy depths, she brought
her never-setting light to Hades
so that her nakedness would abolish Hades;

You too came down to me like this, prepared,
and lay down close to me, mute, motionless,
and Hades was abolished in my heart,
Hades became a resurrection and a triumph,
I held the great pearl in my hand, took spring
into my heart, and felt the scarlet roses
of my fever suddenly become
a crown, felt my black bed become a ship,
the unhurried ship of God, and my struggle
the navigator of my mind among the stars.

Even the Shunammite did not lie like this*
in David's bed to warm his frozen limbs,
David the prophet and king whose spirit now
no longer knew the psalms and in whose heart
was spent that holy virile heat which roused
the king and prophet in him, the fighter,
the dancer, the first defender of God's ark;

δὲν ἐξαπλώθηκε ἔτσι ἡ Σουλαμίτις
πλάι στὸ Δαβίδ, καθὼς Ἐσὺ σιμά μου
σὰν ἡ καρδιά μου βούλιαζε στὸν Ἅδη!

Τὶ Ἐσὺ δὲν ἦρτες μέσ᾽ ἀπὸ τοὺς δρόμους
ὅπου βαδίζουν οἱ θνητοί, νὰ σμίξεις
τοὺς θησαυροὺς τοῦ πόνου μου· ἀλλ᾽ ὡς σμίγουν
σὲ περιπόληση ἄμετρων αἰώνων
δυὸ ἀστέρια, ξάφνου, τό ᾽να πλάι ἀπ᾽ τ᾽ ἄλλο,
κι ἀκέρια ἡ γῆ κι ὁ οὐρανὸς γεμίζουν
στὸ ταίριασμά τους, πλάγιασες σιμά μου,
κι ἅπλωσα τό ᾽να χέρι μου ν᾽ ἀγγίξω
τὸν οὐρανό, κι ἀπ᾽ τ᾽ ἄλλο κάτου ἐπῆρα
γαλήνια τὸ κεφάλι Σου, κι ἀκέρια
γέμισ᾽ ἡ γῆ πλατιὰ ἀπ᾽ τ᾽ ἀγκάλιασμά μας,
κι ἀρμένιζεν ἡ γῆ μέσ᾽ ἀπὸ τ᾽ ἄστρα,
καὶ ψαλμωδοῦσε ἡ γῆ, κι ἀνηφοροῦσε
τοῦ κλιναριοῦ μου ἡ πλώρα πρὸς τὸν πόλο,
συντρίβοντας τὰ κύματα τοῦ χρόνου,
κι ἀρχή, ταξίδι, τέλος, ἦταν ἕνας
κατακλυσμὸς θεϊκοῦ φωτὸς μπροστά μου!

Καὶ νά· ἀπ᾽ τὰ βάθη τοῦ εἶναι μου, ἀπ᾽ τὰ βάθη
ποὺ θεὸς κρυβόνταν στὰ ἰσκερὰ τοῦ νοῦ μου,
τὸ ἱερὸ παραμίλημα λυτρώθη,
κι ἀπὸ τῶν ἴδιων μου σιωπῶν τὸ θάμπος
στροφὲς μεγάλες ξάφνου πλημμυρίσαν
τὰ φρένα μου, γοργὲς στροφές, καὶ λέγαν:

118

even the Shunammite did not lie down
beside David as You lay beside me
that time my heart was sinking into Hades.

Because You did not come to mingle with
the treasures of my pain from streets where mortals walk;
but as two stars circling for countless ages
mingle suddenly, the one beside the other,
and earth and heaven are full at their mating,
so You lay down beside me, and I stretched out
one hand to touch the sky and with the other
gently I held Your head, and the whole earth
filled with our embrace, the earth sailed among
the stars, the earth sang psalms, and my bed's prow
climbed toward the pole, crushing the waves of time,
and beginning, voyage, end, were all
a cataclysm of celestial light before me.

And there, from my being's depths, from the depths
where a god lay hidden in my mind's shadow,
the holy delirium was now set free,
and from the obscurity of my silences
powerful verses suddenly engulfed
my brain, quick verses, and they spoke these words:

« Δὲν εἶν' αὐτὸ γιὰ Σὲ κλινάρι ἀρρώστου,
μὰ ἡ μυστικιὰ τοῦ Διόνυσου τριήρη
ποὺ ἀπάνω ἀπὸ τὰ κύματα τοῦ χρόνου
κι ἀπάνω ἀπ' τοὺς κλειστοὺς Ρυθμοὺς τῆς πλάσης
πετάει γοργή, πετάει μ' ὁρμή, σὰ βέλος!

» Ἄκου τὴ βοὴ τῆς λευτεριᾶς Σου· ἀκέριος
κι ἂν ἔκαιες λίγο πρὶν ἀπὸ τὴ θέρμη,
κι ἂν σὰ δαδὶ φλεγόνταν τὸ κορμί Σου,
νὰ μάθεις ἦταν πῶς νὰ καῖς! Τὶ τώρα
ζυγώνεις τὴ φωτιά, ποὺ ὄχι τὸ πλάσμα
μὰ ὁ ἴδιος Πλάστης ἔχει μὲς στὰ φρένα.
Τ' ἄστρο, ποὺ πλάι Σου λάμπει, εἶναι τῆς Ἥβης,
τῆς αἰώνιας Ἥβης εἶναι τοῦτο τ' ἄστρο,
τ' ἄστρο εἶναι ποὺ τρυπάει τὸ φῶς τῆς μέρας!

» Δὲν εἶσαι πιὰ μ' ὅσα φωτάει ὁ ἥλιος.
Μοιάζεις στὰ βάθη μέσα νά 'σαι τοῦ ἥλιου
ψυχὴ πυρόζωη, μοιάζεις νά 'σαι μέσα
στὸν ἥλιο, κ' εἶν' ἀπόξω, ἀπόξω οἱ φλόγες
ποὺ φωτᾶν τ' ἄλλα ἀστέρια καὶ τὸν κόσμο.
Θωρεῖς τ' ἀστέρια· αὐτὰ δὲ Σὲ θωροῦνε.
Βλέπεις τὸν κόσμο· ὁ κόσμος δὲ Σὲ βλέπει.
Μοιάζεις κρυμμένος ὅλος μὲς στὸν ἥλιο
τοῦ πάθους Σου, κι αὐτοῦθε νὰ τοξεύεις
ἐκεῖ ποὺ δὲν ἀνάτειλαν ἀκόμα
τῆς δημιουργίας τὰ πείσματα! Μελέτη,
μελέτη αὐτὸ θανάτου εἶναι γιὰ Σένα
τὸ πάθος, καὶ μελέτα το ὡς ἀξίζει
στὴ θεία φωτιὰ βαθιά Σου, ποὺ ὄχι ὡς πλάσμα
ἀλλ' ὡς ὁ Πλάστης κλείνεις μὲς στὰ φρένα.

"For You this bed is not a sick man's bed
but the mystical trireme of Dionysus
that flies above the waves of time, above
the closed Rhythms of Creation, flies swiftly,
like an arrow, flies with great force.

Listen to Your freedom's sound; if only now
the whole of You was burning with a fever
and if Your body flamed like pine kindling,
it was so that You could discover how to burn.
Because now You are coming near the fire
that is not in creation but in the mind
of the Creator Himself. The star that shines
beside You is Hebe's, eternal Hebe's,
the star that pierces through the light of day.

You are no longer with what the sun illumines
but seem to be a fire-enkindled soul
in the sun's depths, You seem inside the sun,
and the flames that light the other stars, that light
the world, are now outside, outside of You.
You see the stars; the stars do not see You.
You see the world; the world does not see You.
You seem all hidden in Your passion's sun
and from there You aim Your arrows where
creation's stubbornness has not yet dawned.
For You this passion is a rehearsal for death:
rehearse it as is worthy of the holy fire
deep inside You, that Your mind encloses
not as created but as Creator.

Μελέτη εἶναι θανάτου, ἀρχὴ μεγάλη,
ὕψος καὶ βάθος πιὰ ἐγινῆκαν ἕνα,
ὁ νοῦς Σου εἶναι στὸν Ὄλυμπο, τὸν Ἅδη
γλυκοφωτᾶ ἡ καρδιά Σου. Ἀρχὴ μεγάλη,
τόξο μεγάλο ἐδόθη Σου στὰ χέρια,
καὶ μὴ δειλιᾶς νὰ τὸ τανύσεις, κι ὅλα
τὰ ἐμπόδια νὰ περάσεις μὲ τὸ βέλος
τοῦ πόθου Σου, ὡς νὰ σμίξεις μὲ τὸν ζῶντα
θεόν, ὅπου ἀπ᾽ ἀνάσταση πρὸς ἄλλην
ἀνάστασην ὁρμάει, τὴ μιὰ τὴ σάρκα
γυρεύοντας νὰ πλάσει ἀπάνω ἀπ᾽ ὅλα,
σάρκα ἀπ᾽ τὴ σάρκα του βαθιά, τὸν ζῶντα
θεό, ποὺ ὄχι σὲ μάρμαρο ἢ σὲ στίχο
μὰ στὸ κορμὶ τὸ ἀθάνατο νὰ πάρει
ψυχὴ κι ἀνάστημα ἄξιο τῆς πνοῆς του
πασκίζει πάντα, ἀκοίμητος Τεχνίτης,
μὲς στὴ φωτιὰ τὸν πήλινο ἀνδριάντα
τοῦ ἀνθρώπου, τέλος, πύρινο νὰ πλάσει
ζητώντας.
            Ἄκου ἡ βοὴ τῆς λευτεριᾶς Σου . . .

» Μορφὴ τοῦ πόθου ὁ θάνατος γιὰ Σένα,
καὶ θέριεψέ τον ὡς τὴ λύτρωσή του
ψηλά, θανάτῳ θάνατον πατήσας!

» Πιὰ δὲ Σοῦ λέω: Γιὰ νά 'βγεις ἀπ᾽ τοὺς αἰῶνες,
νὰ γίνεις πρέπει ὁ ἴδιος ἕνας αἰώνας!
Πίσω Σου ὁ κόσμος καίεται σὰν Τρωάδα,
κ᾽ ἡ πυρκαϊά του ἀντιφεγγάει στὰ βάθη
τῶν περασμένων, ὅπως μὲ τὴ δύση
τοῦ ἥλιου ἀντιφεγγᾶν τὰ παραθύρια
μιᾶς πολιτείας ὁλόφλογα καί, ξάφνου,
βυθίζονται στὸ βράδιασμα.

It is a rehearsal for death, a great beginning,
height and depth are one now; Your mind is on
Olympus, Your heart gently illumines Hades.
A great beginning, a great bow has been placed
in Your hands, and do not be afraid
to bend it, so that the arrow of Your longing
wings far beyond all obstacles,
until You join the living god who rises
in one resurrection after another,
striving to create one flesh above all else,
flesh out of his flesh; the living god,
striving always to shape, not in marble
or in verse, but in a deathless body,
a soul and stature worthy of his breath;
sleepless Artificer, seeking through fire
to make the clay statue of man at last
incandescent. Listen to Your freedom's sound . . .

Death for You is now the shape of longing:
nourish it until it rises to the height
of its deliverance, crushing death with death.*

I no longer say to You: to emerge
from the ages You must Yourself become an age.
Behind You the world burns like Troy,
and its burning is reflected deep in things past
as in the sunset the windows of a city
blaze with reflected flames, then suddenly
sink into the coming night.

                              Καὶ πέρα,
καπνοὶ τῆς ἴδιας πυρκαϊᾶς καὶ νέφη,
σιγαναλιώνουν κι ἀργοσβήνουν ὅσα
μελλοντικὰ ἀπ᾽ τὸν ἄνθρωπο λογιοῦνται.
Μὰ 'Εσὺ ὁλοένα λύνεσαι ἀπ᾽ τὸ χρόνο.
"Ασ᾽ τὴν ἀνίδεη καὶ χοντροκομμένη
γενιὰ στοὺς στοχασμούς της, πού 'ναι ψέμα
καὶ πού 'ν' ἐρείπιο, καὶ βυθίσου ἀκέριος
στ᾽ ἄναρχο ρίγος ποὺ χιμάει στὸ νοῦ Σου,
ἀπ᾽ ὅπου δὲν ἀνάτειλαν ἀκόμα
τῆς δημιουργίας τὰ πείσματα, νὰ λάμψει
στὸ κορμὶ καὶ στὸ νοῦ Σου ἡ τέλεια λάμψη
τῆς Σκέψης καὶ τὸ τέλειο Γενηθήτω!»

"Ετσι ὁ Θεὸς ποὺ κρύβεται βαθιά μου,
στὶς ξαφνικὲς μοῦ λύτρωνε στροφές του
τὸ ἱερὸ παραμίλημα, τὴν ὥρα
π᾽ ὅπως ἡ 'Αστάρτη μπαίνοντας στὸν "Αδη,
κι ὅπως ποτὲ δὲ μπῆκε ἡ Σουλαμίτις
στὴν κλίνη τοῦ Δαβίδ, μοῦ πῆρες ξάφνου
καὶ τὸ αἷμα καὶ τὸ πνέμα μου ἀπ᾽ τὴ θέρμη
ποὺ μοῦ 'καιγε τὸ μέτωπο, στὴ θέρμη
τὴ μυστικιά, στὴν τέλεια τοῦ θανάτου
μελέτη, ποὺ τρυπώντας τῆς ἡμέρας
τὴν πλάνη, ὣς χτὲς κλεισμένη στὴν καρδιά μου,
τώρα συντρίβει τοὺς φραγμοὺς τοῦ χρόνου,
σπάει τοὺς φραγμοὺς τῆς μοίρας καὶ τοῦ κόσμου,
κι ἀπάνω κι ἀπ᾽ τὸ χρόνο κι ἀπ᾽ τὴ μοίρα
κι ἀπὸ τὸν κόσμον ὅλο θρονιασμένη,
ἐκεῖ ποὺ δὲν ἀνάτειλαν ἀκόμα
τῆς δημιουργίας τὰ πείσματα, ἀπολύνει,

124

And beyond—
smoke, clouds from the same fire—what man
regards as things to come dissolve slowly
and end in nothing. But You, release Yourself
continually from time. Leave the ignorant
and coarse-cut generation to its thinking:
nothing but lies and debris; plunge wholly
into the immortal shudder
that floods Your mind, where the stubbornness
of creation has not yet dawned, plunge
so that the whole radiance of Thought, the total
'Let there be . . .' lights up Your mind and body."

This way the God who hides deep inside me
set free for me the holy delirium
with his sudden verses, at the moment
when, like Astarte entering Hades—
even the Shunammite never entered
David's bed like that—You suddenly drew
the blood and spirit from the fever burning
my forehead, drew it into this mystical fever,
into the perfect rehearsal for death
that, piercing through the day's deception
locked until yesterday inside my heart,
now shatters the barriers of time,
breaks the barriers of fate and the world;
and enthroned above time and fate, above
the world, where the stubbornness of creation
has not yet dawned, from there releases

125

(ὦ ἄστρο τῆς Ἥβης, τῆς αἰώνιας Ἥβης),
γιὰ μιὰ ἱερὰ ξανανιωμένη πλάση,

(τέλος κι ἀρχὴν ἡ Μνήμη ἐδῶ δὲν ἔχει),

ὠκεανὸ τὴ βοὴ τῆς λευτεριᾶς μου!

(O star of Youth, star of eternal Youth),
for a divinely rejuvenated universe,

(Memory has no end here and no beginning)

the oceanic sound of my freedom!

ΔΙΟΝΥΣΟΣ ΕΠΙ ΛΙΚΝΩ

Νύχτα μεγάλη, νύχτα μάνα μὲς στῶν αἰώνων
τὶς νύχτες, νύχτα κούνια τῶν Τιτάνων
βρεφῶν, π' ἀπόψε ρίχνεις, κι ὅλο ρίχνεις
τὸ χιόνι Σου γοργό, πυκνόν, ἀνάμεσό μου
κι ἀνάμεσα τοῦ κόσμου, κλείνοντάς με
μονάχο στὴν ἀπάτητη σκοπιά μου,
(ὄρθιο κιβούρι, ποὺ μὲ μέλη παγωμένα
βιγλίζω ἀκοίμητος τὰ σύνορα τοῦ χρόνου) ·

Νύχτα - μητέρα, στὴ σιωπή Σου, ἐνῶ λογιάζω
πῶς πάει νὰ σβήσει μὲς στὰ στήθη μου ἡ καρδιά μου
— τὶ ὑπνῶσαν ὅλα, ἡ γῆ στὰ πόδια μου ἀποκάτου,
βαθιὰ τὰ οὐράνι' ἀπάνωθε μου, κι ἀγρυπνάει,
θαρρῶ, στὰ τάρταρα μονάχα ὁ Βύθιος Δράκων,
καὶ πιὰ ἀπ' τὰ χείλη μου μπροστὰ δὲν ἀναφαίνει
μηδὲ τοῦ χνότου μου ὁ ἀχνός, μὰ νὰ τὰ κλείσει
παραμονεύει ὁ θάνατός μου —, αἰφνίδια, λέω
μωροῦ παιδιοῦ πῶς ἀγρικιέμαι κάποιο κλάμα,
ἀλαργινό, τρεμάμενο, κι ἀναρωτιέμαι:
«Τάχα παιδὶ γεννιέται ἀπόψε, πάλι, νέο,
ὁ ἀπ' αἰώνων θεός;»
                    Ἀλλ' ὦ Μητέρα-
νύχτα, μάταια στυλώνω τὴν ἀκοή μου
πίσω ἀπ' τὸ κλάμα αὐτό, μήπως ἀδράξω
στ' αὐτί μου βάβισμα σκυλιῶν μακρὰ σὲ στάνη
τῆς Βηθλεέμ, καὶ μάταια ἀνοίγω τὴ ματιά μου
μὴ δῶ ἀρχαγγέλων σύναξη πυκνὴ ἤ, πιὸ κάτω,
φωτιὰ τσοπάνων νὰ πρυπάει τὰ μαῦρα σκότη.

DIONYSUS ENCRADLED

Great night, mother-night among the nights
of the ages, cradle of the Titans' offspring,
you who pour your snow swift and thick this evening
between me and the outside world, closing me
alone in my unviolated sentry box
(upright coffin where, my limbs frozen, I keep
unsleeping watch on the frontiers of time):

Mother-night, in Your silence, as I feel
my heart waning—for everything sleeps: the earth beneath
my feet, the deep sky above me, and only
the Serpent of the Abyss seems to be awake,
and not even my breath's vapor rises
from my lips, which death waits ready to close—
suddenly I think I hear, low, quavering,
the cry of a baby, and I ask myself:
"Is God, eternal God, being born again
tonight as a young child?"
                                    But, Mother-night,
in vain I strain my ears to catch, behind
this cry, perhaps the sound of dogs moving
in the fold at Bethlehem, and in vain
I strain my eyes to see the angelic host or,
lower down, shepherds' fires piercing the darkness.

Ἀλλ' ὡς τὰ νέφη ἀποσκεπάζονται ἀπὸ νέφη
κι ὅλα τὸ χιόνι σιωπηλὰ τὰ σαβανώνει,
λύκων ἀκούω οὐρλιάσματα νὰ Σὲ γεμίζουν,
θρηνητικά, μακρόσυρτα, στριγκά, μεγάλα,
λύκων ἀκούω γοργὰ κοπάδια νὰ περνᾶνε,
μακρὺς στρατὸς ποὺ διασκελάει μέσ' ἀπ' τὰ χιόνια,
μά, ὡς ξαφνικὰ γυρίζεις πίσω στὴ σιωπή Σου,
ξαναρωτιέμαι τὸ ἴδιο ρώτημα βαθιά μου.

Κι ἀπάντησή μου, ὡς νὰ γκρεμίζεται τὸ τεῖχος
ποὺ μὲ κυκλώνει τῆς σιγῆς σ' ἄγριου στροβίλου
τὸ αἰφνίδιο ξέσπασμα, ντυτοὶ γιὰ σάβανά τους
τὸ ἴδιο τὸ χιόνι ποὺ τὸ χνάρι τους ἐπῆρε,
μύριοι νεκροὶ τριγύραθέ μου, σάμπως μύριοι
φυλακισμένοι ποὺ γκρεμίσανε τὰ τείχη
τῆς φυλακῆς τους, σὰν τρελοὶ ποὺ ξάφνου βρῆκαν
ἀπὸ τὴ θύελλαν ἀνοιχτὴ πλατιὰ μιὰ θύρα
τοῦ ἔρμου σπιτοῦ τους κι ὅλοι ὁρμώντας πρὸς τὴ νύχτα
ἐδιασκορπίσανε στὸ διάστημα, μὲ θρήνους
πνιχτοὺς στὸ κρύφιο τοῦτο ρώτημά μου,
μὲ μιὰ φωνή, λογιάζω, τώρα νὰ μοῦ λένε:
«Παιδὶ γεννιέται ἀπόψε, ἀλήθεια, νέο,
ὁ ἀπ' αἰώνων θεός ... Μὰ ποὺ οἱ φρουροί 'ναι
ποὺ στ' ἅγια σύνορα ἀγρυπνᾶνε, ἀπὸ τοὺς λύκους
νὰ διαφεντέψουνε τὸ βρέφος; Πέ μας, ποῦ εἶναι;»

But as clouds cover the clouds and everything
is wrapped silently in the snow's winding sheet,
I hear—long, doleful, blood-curdling—the howl of wolves
invade you, hear swift packs of wolves go by,
a whole long army climbing through the snow;
yet as once more your silence suddenly fills you,
again I put the same question to myself.

And in answer, as if a whirlwind's savage blast
shatters the wall of silence that enfolds me,
legions of the dead, their winding sheets the same
snow that covers up their tracks, throng all around me,
throng like hordes of prisoners who have smashed
their prison walls, like madmen who have found
suddenly that their asylum door has been burst
wide open by the storm and, pouring out
into the night, have scattered helter-skelter;
and all those dead, grieving, seem to say:
"Truly the eternal God is being born
again tonight as a young child. . . But tell us:
where are the sentinels to keep watch on the sacred
frontiers, to save the child from the wolves?"

131

Τέτοια, λογιάζω, ἀκούω, Μητέρα-νύχτα,
στὰ βάθη μου ἄμετρη φωνή· κι ὡς ἄξαφνα ὅλο
τὸ κοσμογόνο ν' ἀντηχάει τὸ σεῖστρο
μὲς στὴν καρδιά μου, Νύχτα, κούνια τῶν Τιτάνων
βρεφῶν, ἀνεβασμένος στὸν παλμό Σου
τὸ μυστικό, ποὺ κάθε χτύπος του κ' αἰώνας,
στὰ σκότη ὁρμῶ γιὰ νὰ φωνάξω τοὺς συντρόφους,
στὰ σκότη ὁρμῶ, πάνω ἀπ' τὰ χιόνια καὶ τοὺς τάφους,
καὶ, τέτοια λέγοντας στὰ τρίστρατα, τοὺς κράζω:

«Γλυκό μου βρέφος, Διόνυσέ μου καὶ Χριστέ μου·
Τιτάνας νέος κι ἂν ἦρτες σήμερα στὸν κόσμο,
μάνας δὲν ἔχεις ἀγκαλιὰ νὰ Σὲ ζεστάνει...
Τί εἶσαι τῆς νύχτας τούτης γιός, ποὺ μᾶς κυκλώνει,
τῆς νύχτας τούτης καὶ τῆς ἄγρυπνης καρδιᾶς μας
ποὺ, σπίθα ζωῆς μέσα στὸ χάος τὸ παγωμένο,
παλεύει ἀπόψε μὲ τὸ θάνατο τὸν ἴδιο,
δικό μας θάνατο καὶ θάνατο τοῦ κόσμου!
Κι ἄ, τὸ κατέχουμε, π' ἂν ἴσως, νέε Τιτάνα,
ἀπ' τὴν καρδιά μας δὲν πιαστεῖς τὴ νύχτα τούτη,
νά τῆς βυζάξεις στάλα στάλα ὅλο τὸ αἷμα,
αὔριο κ' Ἐσὺ μὲ τοὺς νεκροὺς θὲ νὰ λογιέσαι!
Μὰ κάλλιο τό 'χουμε νὰ μείνουμε θαμμένοι
στὰ ὀρθὰ κιβούρια ποὺ τὰ μέλη μας παγώνουν,
παρὰ ὁ παλμός Σου νὰ σβηστεῖ μὲς στὰ σκοτάδια
μ' ὅλους τοὺς ἄλλους ποὺ πληθαίνουν τὸ κοπάδι
τῆς ἀκατάγραφης ὀργῆς, κ' οἱ ἄγριοι λύκοι
ἀπὸ μακράθε νὰ ὀσμιστοῦνε τὴν κουνιά Σου!

132

This, Mother-night, is the harsh voice I seem to hear
inside me; and as suddenly the whole
world-creating sistrum vibrates in my heart,
I plunge, Night, cradle of the Titans' offspring,
inspired by Your hidden pulse, each beat an age,
into the darkness to summon the companions;
into the darkness I plunge, over snow and tombs,
and with these words I call them at the crossroads:

"My sweet child, my Dionysus and my Christ:
though You have come into the world today, a young Titan,
You have no mother's arms to keep You warm.
For You are the son of the night around us,
of this night, and son of our unsleeping hearts
which, spark of life in the frozen chaos,
fight now with death itself, with our own death
and that of the whole world. And we know,
young Titan, that if You fail tonight to fasten
onto our hearts, to drink their blood drop by drop,
tomorrow You too will be among the dead.
But we hold it better to stay buried
in the upright coffins that freeze our limbs
than for Your pulse to stop in the darkness,
along with all the rest that swell the herd
of indescribable violence, and for savage wolves
from far off to catch the scent of Your cradle.

Μὰ ὡς ἡ κουνιά Σου εἶν' ἡ ἀσπίδα τῶν ἀσπίδων,
κ' ἐμεῖς Κορύβαντες τριγύρα της κινᾶμε
γιὰ νὰ ὀρχηθοῦμε τὸν πυρρίχιο τὸ στερνό μας,
στὴν ἴδια ἀσπίδα μας τὶς σπάθες μας χτυπώντας,
ἀπὸ κοντά Σου ν' ἀποδιώξουμε τοὺς λύκους!
Ὁλονυχτὶς θὲ νὰ ὀρχηθοῦμε γύραθέ Σου,
κι ὅσο κι ἂν εἶναι ἡ νύχτα τούτη νὰ κρατήσει
ἐμεῖς θὰ ὀρχιούμαστε ὣς στὴν ὥρα, ποὺ τὰ σκιάχτρα
τοῦ σκοταδιοῦ θά 'χουνε φύγει, κ' ἡ φωνή Σου,
φωνὴ θεοῦ π' ἀνασηκώνετ' ἀπ' τὸν ὕπνο,
φωνὴ "μεθύοντος ἰσχυροῦ", θὲ νὰ καλέσει
στὴ ζέστα τοῦ ἥλιου ξαφνικὰ τοὺς πεθαμένους,
ἐνῶ ἀποπάνω ἀπὸ τὴν κούνια Σου θὰ γέρνει
ἡ σκιὰ τῆς μιᾶς Σου παντοδύναμης Ἀμπέλου,
γλυκό μας βρέφος, Διόνυσέ μας καὶ Χριστέ μας!»

134

But as Your cradle is the shield of shields,
so we, Corybantes, begin to circle*
around it, to dance our last dance, beating our swords
on our own shields to drive the wolves from You.
The whole night through we'll dance around You,
and however long the night, we'll dance until
the ghouls of the dark have fled, and Your voice—
God's voice that rises out of sleep, voice
of the 'great intoxication'—suddenly calls
the dead into the sun's warmth, while above Your cradle
bends the shadow of Your single mighty Vine,
sweet child, our Dionysus and our Christ."

ΑΓΡΑΦΟΝ

Ἐπροχωροῦσαν ἔξω ἀπὸ τὰ τείχη
τῆς Σιὼν ὁ Ἰησοῦς καὶ οἱ μαθητές Του,
σάν, λίγο ἀκόμα πρὶν νὰ γείρει ὁ ἥλιος,
ζυγώσανε ἀναπάντεχα στὸν τόπο
ποὺ ἡ πόλη ἔριχνε χρόνια τὰ σκουπίδια,
καμένα ἀρρώστων στρώματα, ἀποφόρια,
σπασμένα ἀγγειά, ἀπορρίμματα, ξεσκλίδια . . .

Κ' ἐκεῖ, στὸν πιὸ ψηλὸ σωρὸν ἀπάνω,
πρησμένο, μὲ τὰ σκέλια γυρισμένα
στὸν οὐρανό, ἑνὸς σκύλου τὸ ψοφίμι,
ποὺ—ὡς ξαφνικὰ ἀκούοντας, τὰ κοράκια
ποὺ τὸ σκεπάζαν, πάτημα, τὸ ἀφῆκαν —
μιὰ τέτοια ὀσμὴν ἀνάδωκεν, ὁποὺ ὅλοι
σὰ μ' ἕνα βῆμα οἱ μαθητές, κρατώντας
στὴ φούχτα τους τὴν πνοή, πισωδρομῆσαν . . .

Μὰ ὁ Ἰησοῦς, μονάχος προχωρώντας
πρὸς τὸ σωρὸ γαλήνια, κοντοστάθη
καὶ τὸ ψοφίμι ἐκοίταζε· ἔτσι, πόνας
δὲν ἐκρατήθη μαθητὴς καὶ Τοῦ 'πεν
ἀπὸ μακρά: «Ραββί, δὲ νιώθεις τάχα
τὴ φοβερὴν ὀσμὴ καὶ στέκεσ' ἔτσι ;»

AGRAPHON *

Once at sunset Jesus and his disciples
were on their way outside the walls of Zion
when suddenly they came to where the town
for years had dumped its garbage: burnt mattresses
from sickbeds, broken pots, rags, filth.

And there, crowning the highest pile, bloated,
its legs pointing at the sky, lay a dog's carcass;
and as the crows that covered it flew off
when they heard the approaching footsteps, such a stench
rose up from it that all the disciples, hands
cupped over their nostrils, drew back as one man.

But Jesus calmly walked on by Himself
toward the pile, stood there, and then gazed
so closely at the carcass that one disciple,
not able to stop himself, called out from a distance,
"Rabbi, don't you smell that terrible stench?
How can you go on standing there?"

Κι Αὐτός, χωρὶς νὰ στρέψει τὸ κεφάλι
ἀπ' τὸ σημεῖο ποὺ κοίταζε, ἀποκρίθη:
«Τὴ φοβερὴν ὀσμήν, ἐκεῖνος πόχει
καθάρια ἀνάσα, καὶ στὴ χώρα μέσα
τὴν ἀνασαίνει, ὅθ' ἤρθαμε . . . Μὰ τώρα
αὐτὸ ποὺ βγαίνει ἀπ' τὴ φτορὰ θαμάζω
μὲ τὴν ψυχή μου ὁλάκερη . . . Κοιτάχτε
πῶς λάμπουνε τὰ δόντια αὐτοῦ τοῦ σκύλου
στὸν ἥλιο· ὡς τὸ χαλάζι, ὡσὰν τὸ κρίνο,
πέρα ἀπ' τὴ σάψη, ὑπόσκεση μεγάλη,
ἀντιφεγγιὰ τοῦ Αἰώνιου, μὰ κι ἀκόμα
σκληρὴ τοῦ Δίκαιου ἀστραπὴ κ' ἐλπίδα!»

Ἔτσ' εἶπ' Ἐκεῖνος· κ' εἴτε νιῶσαν ἢ ὄχι
τὰ λόγια τοῦτα οἱ μαθητές, ἀντάμα,
σὰν ἐκινήθη, ἀκλούθησαν καὶ πάλι
τὸ σιωπηλό Του δρόμο . . .

                    Καὶ νά τώρα,
βέβαια στερνός, τὸ νοῦ μου πῶς σ' ἐκεῖνα,
Κύριε, τὰ λόγια Σου γυρίζω, κι ὅλος
μιὰ σκέψη στέκομαι μπροστά Σου: Ἄ! . . . δῶσε,
δὸς καὶ σ' ἐμένα, Κύριε, ἐνῶ βαδίζω
ὁλοένα ὡς ἔξω ἀπ' τῆς Σιὼν τὴν πόλη,
κι ἀπὸ τὴ μιὰ τῆς γῆς στὴν ἄλλην ἄκρη
ὅλα εἶναι ρείπια, κι ὅλα εἶναι σκουπίδια,
κι ὅλα εἶναι πτώματα ἄθαφτα ποὺ πνίγουν
τὴ θεία πηγὴ τ' ἀνασασμοῦ, ἢ στὴ χώρα
εἴτ' ἔξω ἀπὸ τὴ χώρα· Κύριε, δός μου,
μὲς στὴ φριχτὴν ὀσμὴν ὁπού διαβαίνω,
γιὰ μιὰ στιγμὴ τὴν ἄγια Σου γαλήνη,

138

Jesus, His eyes fixed on the carcass,
answered: "If your breath is pure, you'll smell
the same stench inside the town behind us.
But now my soul marvels at something else,
marvels at what comes out of this corruption.
Look how that dog's teeth glitter in the sun:
like hailstones, like a lily, beyond decay,
a great pledge, mirror of the Eternal, but also
the harsh lightning-flash, the hope of Justice!"

So He spoke; and whether or not the disciples
understood His words, they followed Him
as He moved on, silent.

                        And now, Lord, I,
the very least of men, ponder Your words
and, filled with one thought, I stand before You:
grant me, as now I walk outside my Zion,
and the world from end to end is all ruins, garbage,
all unburied corpses choking the sacred
springs of breath, inside and outside the city:
grant me, Lord, as I walk through this terrible stench,
one single moment of Your holy calm,

139

νὰ σταματήσω ἀτάραχος στὴ μέση
ἀπ' τὰ ψοφίμια, καὶ ν' ἀδράξω κάπου
καὶ στὴ δική μου τὴ ματιὰν ἕν' ἄσπρο
σημάδι, ὡς τὸ χαλάζι, ὡσὰν τὸ κρίνο·
κάτι νὰ λάμψει ξάφνου καὶ βαθιά μου,
ἔξω ἀπ' τὴ σάψη, πέρα ἀπὸ τὴ σάψη
τοῦ κόσμου, ὡσὰν τὰ δόντια αὐτοῦ τοῦ σκύλου,
ποὺ, ὦ Κύριε, βλέποντάς τα ἐκειὸ τὸ δείλι,
τά 'χες θαμάσει, ὑπόσκεση μεγάλη,
ἀντιφεγγιὰ τοῦ Αἰώνιου, μὰ κι ἀντάμα
σκληρὴ τοῦ Δίκαιου ἀστραπὴ κ' ἐλπίδα!

so that I, dispassionate, may also pause
among this carrion and with my own eyes
somewhere see a token, white as hailstones,
as the lily—something glittering suddenly
deep inside me, above the putrefaction,
beyond the world's decay, like the dog's teeth
at which that sunset You gazed, Lord, in wonder:
a great pledge, mirror of the Eternal, but also
the harsh lightning-flash, the hope of Justice!

NOTES

7 The horses of Achilles, Balius and Xanthus, were immortal, a wedding gift from Poseidon to Achilles' father, Peleus.

9 Cf. Plutarch, *Life of Lycurgus*, xv, 6-7: "After giving marriage such traits of reserve and decorum, he none the less freed men from the empty and womanish passion of jealous possession, by making it honourable for them, while keeping the marriage relation free from all wanton irregularities, to share with other worthy men in the begetting of children, laughing to scorn those who regard such common privileges as intolerable, and resort to murder and war rather than grant them. For example, an elderly man with a young wife, if he looked with favour and esteem on some fair and noble young man, might introduce him to her, and adopt her offspring by such a noble father as his own." Trans. Bernadotte Perrin, *Plutarch's Lives* (London, 1928) vol. I, pp. 251-53.

11 The Doric Apollo is the central figure in a pediment of the temple of Zeus at Olympia.

13 The castle is that crowning Mistra, on the hillside above Sparta.

15 Acrocorinth is the name of the steep and solitary mountain (1,900 feet in height) that served as the citadel of ancient Corinth.
The meltemi is the term given a local northwest wind, common in the heat of summer throughout Greece.
Pegasus, the winged horse who ascended to the seat of the immortals and carried thunder and lightning for Zeus, was associated with Corinth and often represented on the coins of this city-state.

17 Salona is the popular name for the town of Amfissa, whose port is Itea, on the Corinthian Gulf.

19 The scene described is that of the Panathenaic procession from the "Zooforos" frieze of the Parthenon.

21 Cymothoe and Glauce were among the Nereids, daughters of Nereus, a sea divinity.

143

27   The primary allusion is to Salamis as the visible con-
      temporary island in the Saronic Gulf.
      Kineta is a beach on the Saronic Gulf between Eleusis
      and Corinth, now a tourist center but beautifully tree-
      lined and virtually deserted at the time the poem was
      written.
29   Pan, the Greek god of shepherds and their flocks, was
      normally represented as partly goatlike in shape.
31   Thalero (Vernal) is a village on the Corinthian Gulf
      near one of the poet's residences in Sykia, in the neighbor-
      hood of Xilokastron.
37   Boccaccio narrates a related dream by Dante's mother in
      his *Life of Dante*, xvii. He recounts that the mother gave
      birth to her son under a lofty laurel tree, and her son,
      feeding on laurel berries from this tree and drinking
      water from a clear spring nearby, grew to become a great
      shepherd. Reaching for a leafy laurel branch, the son
      appeared to fall, and Dante's mother suddenly seemed to
      see not him but a peacock. The marvel of this transforma-
      tion woke her. Boccaccio goes on to offer his interpretation
      of the dream.
45   "The Village Wedding" presupposes the following tradi-
      tional pattern for the wedding described (the pattern varies
      throughout Greece in some of its details, depending on the
      character of local communities): The bridegroom gathers
      his party (relatives and close friends), and they travel to
      the bride's village on horseback and muleback. In her
      village, the bride prepares herself for the wedding cere-
      mony and for her permanent departure. The bridegroom
      meets her at her home and, after the ceremony takes
      place, escorts her to her new home in his village. The
      honey and the pomegranate with which the bridegroom's
      mother annoints the new threshold are symbols of good
      luck and fertility.
67   The imagery and allusions in this poem derive in large part
      from the cult of Artemis Orthia and her sanctuary on the
      banks of the Eurotas in Laconia, close to ancient Sparta
      and beneath the "bronze mountain" of Taygetus. Artemis
      Orthia was a goddess of the hunt, of the fertility of both
      human beings and beasts, and of childbirth. She was

144

associated at times with the moon, with the night, with Apollo and Aphrodite. The name Orthia—"upright" or "standing"—has been variously interpreted: it may have been given to the goddess because she made those who served her stand upright; it may have had a phallic significance; or it may have referred to the upright archaic form of her idol, honored at times by torch-races and by human sacrifice. The idol was said to have been brought back by Orestes from the land of the Tauroi and, on reaching Laconia, it caused civil strife and plague. An oracle told the people that to end this they must wet the altar in the shrine with human blood. According to Pausanias, victims for sacrifice were chosen by lot until Lycurgus introduced the rite of scourging young men— "and so the altar continued to be stained with gore." All young Spartans were scourged; the priestess of Orthia stood by, holding the idol of the goddess, which, if the beating were not severe enough, became extremely heavy. Often the victim died under the scourging, while a prize, probably a wreath, was given to him who could endure most. Plutarch (or his authority) thought that this was part of a moral training, especially suitable for future soldiers; others, e.g., Frazer, and Sikelianos in this poem, regard it as part of a ceremony of initiation and purification.

69 The allusion is to Prometheus.
83 See the note to p. 21 above.
    Taenarum is on the coast south of Sparta. Located here is the entrance to Hades from which Hercules dragged up Cerberus.
89 Daedalus was the mythical figure under whose name the Athenians and Cretans personified the earliest development of the arts of sculpture and architecture. Among Daedalus's works were the wooden cow that concealed Pasiphaë, the labyrinth at Knossos that contained the Minotaur, and the wings that brought his son Icarus to tragedy but allowed Daedalus to escape the wrath of Minos and fly free to Sicily.
99 The Sacred Way is the ancient road by which the great Iakchos procession went from Athens to Eleusis for the celebration of the Eleusinian Mysteries.

107   Arion was the name of a fabulous horse fathered by Poseidon.

Eleusis was the home of the Eleusinian Mysteries (see note to p. 99 above).

115   The term *rehearsing* is adapted from Plato's *Phaedo* (see 67e and 80d-81a; the original has been variously translated as "practicing death," "training to die," and "the cultivation of dying").

117   David and the Shunammite (termed Shulamite by Sikelianos) appear in 1 Kings 1:1-4: "Now king David was old and stricken in years; and they covered him with clothes, but he gat no heat. Wherefore his servants said unto him, Let there be sought for my lord the king a young virgin: and let her stand before the king, and let her cherish him, and let her lie in thy bosom, that my lord the king may get heat. So they sought for a fair damsel throughout all the coasts of Israel, and found Abishag a Shunammite, and brought her to the king. And the damsel was very fair, and cherished the king, and ministered to him: but the king knew her not."

123   The phrase "crushing death with death" is taken from the resurrection hymn sung on Easter Sunday in the Greek Orthodox Church.

135   The Corybantes were companions—sometimes eunuch priests—of the Asiatic goddess Cybele. The Corybantes accompanied the goddess with music and wild dances. They were also associated by some ancient authorities with the Cretan Curetes, lovers of dance and sport, who, under instructions from Rhea, concealed the infant Zeus from Cronus, drowning its cries with the sound of their clashing weapons.

137   The term agraphon, literally "unwritten thing," designates a saying or tradition about Christ either not recorded in the Gospels or incapable of being traced to its original source. A related parable is found in the Persian poet, Nizami (1141-1203) and was adapted by Goethe for inclusion in his "Noten und Abhandlungen" appended to *West-Östlicher Divan*.

BIOGRAPHICAL DATA

The following is based in large part on "Chronology of His Life and Work" in *Sikelianos: 1884-1951*, ed. Yerasimos Grigoris, Society of Lefkadian Studies, Athens, 1971.

1884   Born on March 15 in the town of Lefkada on theIonian island of that name, the youngest of seven children. His family had a longstanding association with the island and were friends of the well-known Lefkadian poet Aristotle Valaoritis. Sikelianos's father was a teacher of French.

1885   His paternal home burned to the ground, causing the family to move to rented quarters on the seafront. His parents' income, largely from inheritance, gradually declined in the years following.

1891-95   Attended the Lefkada Elementary School and the Greek School of Lefkada.

1900   Completed the four-year course at the Lefkada Gymnasium, receiving his diploma at the age of sixteen.

1901   Moved to Athens and enrolled in the Law School of Athens University (he did not finish the course). Joined the group that had formed the New Theatre of Constantine Christomanou, as did his sisters Penelope and Helen. At this time Penelope met and eventually married Raymond Duncan, brother of Isadora Duncan, who introduced her—and, at a later date, Sikelianos—to theatre groups in Paris.

1902   Published his first poems in Athenian literary periodicals of the time.

1905-7   At Penelope Duncan's home in Athens, Sikelianos met Eva Palmer of New York, who became his first wife and lifelong supporter. Sikelianos returned from a trip to Libya in 1906 to accompany Eva to America, where they were married in September of 1907, at Bar Harbor, Maine.

147

1909 Sikelianos published his first volume of poems, *Alafroiskiotos* (which included "Return" and "The Horses of Achilles"). The volume immediately established him as an important new voice in Modern Greek poetry. A son, Glafkos, born to Eva (Sikelianos's only child).

1911-12 Trips to France and Italy. He and Eva participated in a Paris production of *Electra* in the original, met Rodin, returned to Athens in the summer before the Balkan War broke out. Sikelianos enlisted as a soldier and served in mainland Greece and Epirus. He began at this time to publish prolifically and continued to do so throughout much of his life.

1914-15 Met Nikos Kazantzakis in Athens and became his intimate friend. The two toured Athos together for forty days in November and December of 1914, and they traveled to a number of Classical and Byzantine sites in Greece during 1915.

1917-19 Years spent mostly in Athens (including Kifissia), with extended visits to Spetses and the Mani in the company of Kazantzakis.

1920 Settled with Eva in the village of Sykia on the Corinthian Gulf.

1921 In April, traveled to Palestine to visit the holy sites. In October, along with other Greek intellectuals, Sikelianos signed an appeal on behalf of the suffering peoples of Russia.

1923 Planned a series of twenty lectures for the School of Law at Athens University on the ancient and modern forefathers of the idea of world freedom and brotherhood, but he delivered only the first two of these.

1924 With his wife Eva as the lead promoter, Sikelianos took the first steps toward organizing an International Delphic Center and a Delphic University, projects that were to occupy the couple more or less continually during the following decade and that were ultimately unsuccessful. The first gathering of some one hundred potential sponsors in Athens was not propitious; Eva is reported to have said: "We might as well have been

148

talking to puppets. Already at that time the Delphic project was a mockery in Athens."

1925   In April, a second meeting of Greek and foreign intellectuals to discuss the proposed International Delphic Center. In June, Sikelianos returned to Lefkada—along with the leading poet of Greece at the time, Kostis Palamas—to take part in the festivities honoring the centennial of Valaoritis's birth.

1926-27 The Delphic projects crystallized into the Delphic Festival, which took place in May of 1927, with theatrical and dance productions, concerts, athletic games, and handicraft exhibits, mostly under the direction of Eva. In order to help defray the debts incurred, Sikelianos mortgaged his villa in Sykia.

1928-29 Years devoted largely to planning and fund raising for the second Delphic Festival. Sikelianos traveled to Paris twice in this connection. He and Eva were awarded silver medals by the Academy of Athens "for their courageous effort to resurrect the Delphic games."

1930   Second Delphic Festival in May, with productions of Aeschylus' *Prometheus Bound* and *The Suppliants*, craft exhibits, and athletic games.

1931   Sikelianos invited to attend the International Symposium at Lucerne. Also invited to Paris, where he met Paul Valéry, among other French men of letters. In the fall, visited Eleusis to do research on the Eleusinian Mysteries.

1933   Two performances of his tragedy, *Dithyramb of the Rose*, on Philopappou Hill in Athens. In August, Eva returned to America and was advised by her brother that her inheritance had been dissipated by expenses in Greece. Though she continued to promote the "Delphic Idea" in America and also to send some funds to her husband, she did not return to Greece until the year after his death, in 1952 (she died that year and was buried at Delphi).

1934-37 For Sikelianos, years of increasing disillusionment with prospects for the "Delphic Idea," which was no

149

longer supported by the Greek government or other sources, local and foreign. The poet became more and more isolated, and his financial situation remained insecure at best. During this period he began to develop his mature, tragic voice.

1938-40 His son Glafkos joined his mother in America, never to return to Greece during the poet's lifetime. In March of 1938, Sikelianos met his second wife, Anna Karamani, in Athens and again in Pelion, where he rented a village house. They were married in Eleusis in June 1940, following the termination of his marriage to Eva.

1941-42 Moved with Anna to an apartment in Athens near the Stadium, the couple hard pressed by the catastrophic first winter of the German-Italian Occupation. In February of 1942, again met Kazantzakis after a long hiatus in their friendship. Spent May to October on the island of Aigina, where Kazantzakis also rented a house.

1943 Was a pallbearer at the funeral of Palamas. Sikelianos's health began to deteriorate at this time. Beyond party or political considerations, he supported the resistance movement until Greece's liberation.

1944-47 Years of growing—though still limited—international recognition. Some of his poems translated into French, Italian, and English. In 1946, the Society of Greek Writers nominated him for the Nobel Prize, along with Kazantzakis. In December of the same year, Sikelianos lectured on Keats at the British Council in Athens. In May of 1947, elected President of the Society of Greek Writers.

1948-49 In retirement in his apartment near the Stadium, with frequent visits to the island of Salamina (Salamis). In April of 1949, lectured on Shakespeare's *The Tempest* at the British Council.

1950 Suffered a stroke in May. Moved to Kifissia in August to convalesce. No longer able to walk.

1951 Nominated for a place in the Academy of Athens, but the members of the Academy failed to elect him. He died on June 19, some days after drinking Lysol, which his maid had mistakenly brought him in place of Nujol.

THE LOCKERT LIBRARY OF POETRY
IN TRANSLATION

LIBRARY OF CONGRESS CATALOGING IN PUBLICATION DATA

Sikelianos, Angelos, 1884-1951
  Selected poems.

  (Lockert library of poetry in translation)
  I. Keeley, Edmund.   II. Sherrard, Philip.
PA5610.S5A24   889'.1'32   79-84017
ISBN 0-691-06405-9
ISBN 0-691-01362-4 pbk.